THIRTY DAYS AND CHANGE

STEVEN BROWNING

SELF-PUBLISHED BY STEVEN BROWNING | 2019

1

SETTING THE STAGE

Thirty Days of Change is a way to transform yourself from where you are currently to where you would like to be. In this book, I will teach you how to build a plan that suits you and is effective in leading you, even when you are lost. I don't ask you to bend to what I want, I ask you to decide what you want and show you how to get it. I use the thirty-day challenge method and I ask you to either form a new good habit or give up a negative old habit, your choice.

Why would I ask you to handle the pressure of changing your life at the same time I ask you to form or delete a habit? Because it creates balance and it takes balance to change your life.

The thirty-day challenge is a self-challenge in which we choose something to start or stop doing for thirty days, consecutively. We can choose to stop smoking, drinking, watching television or anything else we want to eliminate from our lives. We can also choose to start doing something that positively affects our lives. We may choose to start running daily, reading books or even helping others daily. Whatever you choose to do or not do, make sure you are challenging yourself and being realistic for a first-time challenge.

I have completed many thirty-day challenges and have not broken one yet. My first challenge was to run every day for thirty days straight. Each day of the challenge was an entirely new experience. I recorded the details of each day and I will be sharing my experiences with you along your journey. I wrote about my first challenge in my blog during my second challenge. My intent with this book is to help others have the same success with the thirty-day challenge as I have had. I will talk a little more later about why the thirty-day challenge is so important to me.

If I can expose a trap or motivate someone enough to help them through one of the challenges they will face, I will consider this a success. I know there have been many days where the voices in my head were against me. Asking me what I expected to accomplish and who do I think I am? Why am I doing this? When the challenge gets tough, our minds work in a few different ways.

First, our minds will try to magnify our task and make it seem impossible. I call this mentality the "it's too hard" mentality. There is no way I can finish this challenge, so why not quit now and save my effort and pain? We tell ourselves things like "others won't even attempt something like this because they are smarter than me and know better than to waste their time". These are the things our minds try to tell us to keep us from the pain of failure. While our mind has our own best interests in mind, our hearts have our best efforts in mind. How great can I be if I give it my all? What If I were to make it past my mental limitations and reach for the stars, what would happen? These are the questions our heart asks us.

In order to hear our hearts, we must practice listening to them. The words of the heart can be faint at first. They may be mere whispers, after all, our hearts aren't used to being heard. We normally do what we think and what we think is "how do we stay safe and good?". Our hearts will teach us to take chances and become great, if we are willing to listen.

After we beat the "its too hard" mentality, our minds will try a different approach. I call this one the "it doesn't matter" mentality. You know this doesn't even matter. Even if you complete this challenge, you will still be the same person so what is the point? Even if you fight your whole life to be great, you will still be in a wooden box when you die, just like the people that do nothing every day, so why bother? But we know what we want, and we are not only willing to do the work, we are eager to do it. We crave the pain. Each time we push as hard as we can, we are in awe because we went so much farther than we did the last time. Do this enough and we become engaged.

When we are engaged, we are an unstoppable force. Things that we once considered road blocks are merely a small bump in the road. We can take these bumps and never miss a step. We move and grow at a faster pace because we are making intentional moves. We are taking calculated steps, and this leaves little room to stumble. When we do stumble, we recover easily and keep going forward.

My intent for this book - To help you become engaged via the thirty-day challenge. Not only will this help you finish you challenges but it turns out that thirty days is just the amount of time it takes to become good at doing something or to become good at not doing something. Thirty days has been a key number for me and I'm here to help it become a keystone in the arch of your personal and professional growth.

These thirty-day challenges, when chosen right, will push you to reach past your limits. You will reach new limits and use the same method to break through those limits. How far can you go? How much can you learn? How many bad habits can you break that you once thought impossible? It depends on the amount of effort you are willing to spend and the way you handle yourself each day of the challenge.

I am writing this guide with **your** thirty-day challenge in mind. My focus is directly aimed at exposing the traps you will encounter along the way, keeping you motivated through the doubtful moments and providing relevant personal stories that show how I made it through. Thirty days is all it takes to change the way you see yourself, your attitude and your life. Take a trip with me through my first thirty-day challenge and see what it did for me.

2

DAY ONE

THE MORNING

I t's day one of your challenge, and you may not be taking it very seriously at this point. You may be thinking that nothing seems different. I'm going to eventually smoke a cigarette just like I did all the times I've quit before. I'm not going to run every day for thirty days, why would I do it? What is going to stop me from smoking? What is going to make me run? What is there to physically stop me from eating that candy? This guide doesn't come with any nicotine gum to help me so what is it going to do? I'm asking you to keep an open mind and trust that you will stick to this challenge. Why? Because you have accepted a challenge by one of the most important people in the world and we just don't back away from challenges like that.

This challenge doesn't own you, but you do own this challenge. I will be walking you through the hard times as we go along on a day by day timeline but feel free to jump around, if you find something that helps.

As you prepare to face day one, I'd like to walk you through an exercise that I use often. This exercise has helped me to handle many tough moments in my life as well as my career. I use this when I need to relieve stress, when I need to be my best and when I have an over-whelming task or feeling.

Go to a place where you can be alone and take a few minutes to sit silently. Now take a few really deep breaths and close your eyes on your last exhale. If there is background noise, then focus on that noise for a moment and then turn you focus back to your breath, letting the noise become more of a background noise. Ask yourself why you started this challenge? Think about what you will gain when you make it through this challenge. Imagine the feeling of actually making it through this challenge and knowing without a doubt that you can do it. Let that feeling soak in for a moment.

Now imagine for a second that you were to give in right now. Just give in and take the easy road, smoke that cigarette or eat the bad food or not go for the run. Will it feel better? Maybe for about five minutes but how about after that? I can confidently tell you from experience that the pain and discomfort that you are feeling right now, as you fight, are nothing compared to the self-torture and feeling of being weak. It may be easier to sit on the couch than it is to run but sitting there mentally kicking yourself in the ass is much harder than running.

Now, it's time to deal with that pain and discomfort. Focus in on your pain and ask yourself if you are stronger than the pain. If the answer is yes then keep on going but at any time, if the answer is no then you will need to dissect that pain to a level where you can see what it is made of. Ask yourself why that pain is stronger than you? What exactly is that pain made of? Do I own this pain or does it own me? Do I really want to hear myself say that I am weak?

When you finish the steps above, open your eyes and just sit still for a moment before moving on. While you are sitting, take time to see how "being in control" feels and save that feeling so you can come back to it when you need to.

If you still feel like you aren't strong enough then try to substitute something healthy or do something else to keep your focus where you need it. If you gave up cigarettes, then try eating something healthy to compensate. If you are running, allow yourself to think about something that you have been avoiding or slow down and regain control. Its all about keeping yourself from doing what you have always done on day one.

The Afternoon

The afternoon brings a new set of challenges. You made it through a tough morning and the evening will be tough as well, but you will be tougher. The afternoon brings feelings of satisfaction that we don't necessarily need to accept, yet. There is an old saying that says "never congratulate yourself on a job half done". We want to ensure that we stay solid throughout the entire day. Our minds will tell us that we made it through the morning, we deserve a reward. The truth is that rewards are given to us all along the way, but the congratulation comes at the end. We also benefit from every second that we spend challenging ourselves.

When you catch your mind offering you a congrats too early, rein it in and remember that you can do this. Pay attention to the traps that the mind will set for you. When you start asking yourself "why am I doing this" or other negative questions, be ready, it's a trap. These traps are hard to see when you are fighting off urges and cravings. Your mind is already busy, so it can be easy to step in these traps.

When you are approaching a trap or think you may have your foot on a land mine, just relax and give yourself a moment. Think again of why you started this challenge and how it will feel when you finish. Also think again about how you will feel if you give in. Imagine for a few seconds that you did give in. I quit, and I don't have to accomplish anything. Now what? Are you going to just go back to the way you were? No way. Why not? because you will have lost a little respect for yourself. You will know that you could have done better but you didn't. Directly after that sense of relief comes a horrible feeling of regret. Ask yourself how tough am I? Do you know the answer? I doubt it because I believe we are as tough as we need to be. I remember when I was a kid, I would watch and read about "The Hulk". When faced with a threatening situation, The Hulk would rise up and become a big green beast that could handle anything. Even when it seemed impossible for the Hulk to win, he would grow even larger and overcome the situation. When the threat was eliminated, he would calm down and become a man again. There were times when it looked like The Hulk was surely beaten but he always came back and prevailed. During the beginning of this challenge, I need you to be a big green beast. When your cravings, urges and other things seem like they will overcome you, grow larger and overcome. I always knew The Hulk would win and I know you will too. The Hulk was a cartoon when I watched it as a kid but even then, it inspired me to overcome the challenges I faced. After we make it through these first few days, you may be able to go back to being a simple human but for now, I need the beast.

When we give up, we know in our hearts that we didn't try our very best. We know we could have done it, but we were too lazy to own our mind. It's not weakness but laziness that often defeats us. Do this often enough and it will become a habit. Keep this bad habit long enough and it will become a culture. This is the stuff losers are made of and you aren't here to become a loser, so you will survive today, and you will do it again tomorrow. You will find a way to beat the "I don't want to" that will be there to wake up with you.

Tomorrow, you will rise and fight this challenge with everything you have. You will do this again because there is a little light that is starting to shine in your mind. A flame that is small, but it just might possibly be growing. This flame is called determination and its likely very weak at this moment. Inside this flame is everything you have ever wanted. Every desire you have ever had is inside this flame and all you must do is help it stay burning and growing.

While you are tending your flame, be sure to protect it from the wind. The wind comes from others that question your challenge. Why would you do that to yourself? You are crazy to be up at four am running in the rain just because you challenged yourself. You are too hard on yourself. What is wrong with you? The wind will tell you stories about themselves that will attempt to discourage you. They will compare themselves to you and your challenges and find a million ways that you can't do this.

The wind often comes from the people that are closest to you so be ready for them. I find that the best way to keep loved ones from blowing out your flame is to tell them how important it is to you. If they don't see it, its because its not meant for them, it's meant for you. I find that the best way to deal with negative wind, that isn't from a loved one is to acknowledge them and leave it alone. Don't try to argue your position on the matter, just simply move on. You don't need to waste time arguing about anything negative. Instead, set an example by leaving a trail of positivity behind you.

3

A STORY FROM MY OWN DAY ONE

O n day one of my first challenge, I took the whole challenge thing lightly. Here I am, running along at five am and I think to myself, sure you are going to do this every day for thirty days. Sure, you won't miss a day. What are you going to do when work calls for travel? I tell myself to just give it a chance. I can always quit later, if I want to. What is going to stop me from quitting? Nothing, so I will just run and worry about the commitment part later. It's important to know that I have been a runner for a long time, but I haven't run consistently in over a year at this time.

It's important because I don't want you to think I took a huge challenge as my first one. I was a runner in the past so I'm somewhat familiar with the pains of running and getting back into it. This time, however, there would be no rest or healing periods for thirty days.

As I'm running on day one, I wonder if I shouldn't have chosen something a little harder. I easily make the duration that I wanted to run and I'm feeling pumped up, so I keep running. I am amazed at how good I'm feeling and can't wait to get up and do it again in the morning. As you read this, I'm sure you already know that this feeling would not last...

4

DAY TWO

THE MORNING

On day two of your challenge, you may still not have completely committed to this challenge. You are still focusing on what you are sacrificing and not what you are gaining. The morning of day two can be a little harder than it was on day one because your urges and pain are still full strength and you are tired from fighting day one. Don't panic, day two is one of the hardest days of the challenge. Decide right now to be the big green beast and overcome whatever challenges you face. Think again about that feeling of regret that we have when we quit before the finish. That feeling is worse than the pain and effort you must endure in order to make it through day two.

When you start feeling those urges, go back to that place we talked about on day one. The quiet place where you can close your eyes and turn noise and pain into peace and strength. While you are in this place, realize that the cravings and urges will start to fade on day three. You only must endure this amount of pressure for the rest of today. I would like to tell you that this will make it easier, but the truth is that it will be hard to make it through the morning of day two. Again, the important thing is to remain calm and let the pain and urges pass. Don't try to ignore them, instead, dissect them. Tear them apart and determine what makes them so strong. Once you figure out that your own mind is what gives the pain and urges their power, all you must do is decide to be stronger than them. Ask yourself the following questions. Why do I feel it? What power does it have over me? If I give in to it, will I be happy? Do this as soon as the pain and urges enter your mind. They have a way of coming on subtle at first and then growing into something that is very hard to control. Remember that the pain and urges have power only if you give it to them. You are the only controller of your actions. No cigarette, junk food or laziness has the right to control what you do.

The Afternoon

On the afternoon of day two, you will again want to congratulate yourself on getting through the first day and a half. It is ok to give yourself a quick fist bump but don't overdo it. We still have a long way to go and your determination flame hasn't grown to strong enough yet. Be happy that you made it this far but be aware that the day isn't over yet. Think ahead for a minute of how great it will be to make a new habit or break an old one. This is the cost of admission for that feeling, it's as simple as that. There is no magic button but there is magic in you and if you keep pushing toward what you want, you will find it.

As afternoon tiredness kicks in and the evening's batch of pain and urges come washing over you, try beating them by doing something new. After all, you will be a different person after this challenge is over so why not take advantage of the situation? What would you want this new person to be doing right now?

This is a chance to begin creating the person you have always wanted to be. Remember the flame that is growing? Well, now is the time to start preparing for when that small flame becomes a fire. What do you have to burn? What are you going to feed that fire with? How will you find new and better ways to cultivate that flame? What will you do with yourself when your flame is burning so hot that others are afraid of it? Take a moment to let that sink in and then write down these questions or email them to yourself. Whatever will ensure that you see them often. Add any other self-questions that you think of and capture them the same way.

The answers to these questions will be ever changing so don't think that you need to be rigid. Whenever you feel an urge or pain that you are trying to beat, take one of these questions and start finding the answer to it. It's ok to change these answers often as you grow and evolve but it is imperative that you start coming up with answers. Remember to add questions that will inspire your future, as they arise. We will be adding questions daily, answering them and checking on our flame often from this point forward.

As the afternoon fades into evening and you wind down for the day, remember that tomorrow is the day when these urges will begin to weaken. Tomorrow is the day that you will begin to take the upper hand. Why? Because you have made it through two of the hardest parts of the challenge. Starting and continuing. Just before you fall asleep for the night, take a quick assessment of your determination flame. Has it grown? Is it being affected by the wind? Remember to assess your flame every night as you fall asleep.

5

A STORY FROM MY OWN DAY TWO

A s I ran on day two, I started off with a little soreness, but it quickly went away. I wondered again if I pushed myself hard enough on this challenge. I decided to give it till the end of the week and if it were still too easy, I would increase my minimum run time. After all, I wanted this to be something that was hard to achieve.

After I finished overthinking and second guessing my durations, I took some time to pay attention to the day and my surroundings. It was a beautiful day and I had time to wonder why I ever stopped running in the first place. I was feeling great, I had almost zero pain and the universe seemed to be slanting the world so that my run was all downhill. Again, I thought to myself, why wouldn't everyone do this every day? Who wouldn't want to be a part of this every day?

After my run, I finished off the day with some physical labor on one of the projects I had been working on. I felt unstoppable. I was putting in the effort and feeling results. I thought to myself, so this is how it's supposed to work. This is simple, why did I make it so complicated in the past?

To be clear, when you are implementing a positive habit, day two is fairly easy but when you are eliminating a bad habit, day two is pretty tough. In fact, I would say that day two is the hardest day when you are throwing out a bad habit. If I was forced to call out a "hardest day" of starting a positive habit, I would say it is day fourteen. On day fourteen, you are tired and still have over half-way to go. In short. when you commit to performing an action daily, it takes a while for it to become a challenge, while stopping a bad habit is an immediate challenge that fades as time passes.

6

DAY THREE

THE MORNING

On the morning of day three you will likely feel a small victory for surviving day two that will be impossible to completely deny. Again, give yourself a small pat on the back but don't congratulate yourself too much. We don't want yesterday's victory to get in the way of today's efforts. Take a moment to recap over the last two days. Feel that pain one last time before you let it go because each day is different, and you only get to experience that exact pain once. There will be plenty of new pain ahead but never that exact one.

I said before, that the urges and pain will begin to fade by today and they will. The change may be subtle but it's there and you survived yesterday's stronger temptations so today may be slightly easier. You have overcome your urges for the last forty-eight hours and this challenge is starting to become a real thing. The value of quitting a bad habit or forming a healthy habit is starting to become clear.

You begin to realize that finishing this challenge is valuable, but you still may not be committed. Your mind will try to keep you safe from greatness. Your mind may be saying things like "look at how tired you are of fighting pain and urges already, think about how you will feel thirty days from now". You struggled through but how long are you willing to struggle? Forever? These thoughts your mind will throw at you are designed to stop you from putting yourself through this challenge. You may have other forces that are trying to help you quit this challenge, as well. Possibly close friends or relatives that don't believe in themselves. These people will often unintentionally project their weaknesses on you and you need to be aware enough to recognize this. When you understand that you aren't limited by the limitations of others, their opinion becomes powerless. I like to call the doubt from others, "the wind". I call it this because it is constantly trying to blow out your flame of determination.

The wind may increase as it becomes clear that you are serious about your challenge. Remember that others don't like to feel like they will be left behind. Loved ones may be afraid that you will see them as less valuable when you become a better person. Assure them that you are trying to do better and that you will help them become better as well. Remember that your flame can still be blown out so be cautious. The greatest thing in the world is helping others but it is a tragedy when you try to help someone up and they pull you down instead.

Along with the wind and your mind, other forces may be working against you. Maybe Murphy's law is proving itself to you. Maybe a few negative things are happening around you and you think that you would feel better if you just smoked a cigarette or gave in to other urges. Or maybe you have the greatest excuse in the world for not going running this morning, but are you going to use that excuse? No! Why? Because you have endured this pain for a long two days and you need to get a reward for it. If you quit now, there is no reward but when you make it, the reward is amazing. The reward is the person you will become as you work to be better.

As we keep moving through this challenge, I will show you how I became the person I wanted to be and I will help you be the person you want to be. Of course, you will still be you, but you will be become a better version of you. You will become a version of yourself, which is already a great version, that is self-disciplined. I will not be the judge of whether you are a better version of yourself, you will. I want you to decide what that person looks, acts and feels like.

The Afternoon

On the evening of day three, you are beginning to feel the small change in the urges and pain. The pain and urges are still there and making noise but there is a small numbness to it. It's almost like they are filtered. At some point, you will realize that the urges and pain aren't weaker or diluted but you have become stronger and your self-discipline has increased. Over the last two and a half days, you have also increased your tolerance to pain. In less than three days, you have enhanced your ability to control your own mind. To resist the things, you want or don't want. Many of us never develop these abilities. We wander through life and allow every pain, urge or the wind to determine what we do and even what we think. Not you though, you have made it through the part where even the strong usually quit and that says a lot about you. More on this later but for now, keep going!

It is important that you keep your sense of victory in check because the temptation is far from over. Enjoy the feeling of your newly honed character but don't think that it will be easy. In fact, there are still many weak moments to come that will test you in so many ways and you will need to deal with that.

When the urges become strong enough that you fear you might give in, remember to go to that quiet place in your head and have a moment for yourself. While you are in that place, think about how the urges have faded a little. Compare how you expected it to feel vs how it feels right now. Is it how you expected? Of course not, because the cravings are what we make them to be and in this hard moment, you are letting them tempt you. Urges, pain, fear and other emotions exist in our heads. They can be strong, but the truth is that they are in our control, if we decide to control them.

Often, we don't even attempt to control our minds at all, so we do whatever we think we want at the time. We pass by something that looks desirable and think we want it, so we get it. Once we get it, did it make us happy? Advertising uses the power of suggestion to get your attention and plant a seed. That seed quickly grows into an urge and guess what happens next. We eat it, smoke it or whatever the case may be, but does it really do what we thought it would do? Do you feel better about yourself when you give in to your urges or pain? No. Why? Because we only thought we really wanted it because we were sold on it. We allow the seeds that grow to be planted by every internal emotion and by outside forces. This may not apply directly to your challenge but it's important to realize that our minds may work this way. Eric Thomas says "the gazelle stops running when the lion isn't chasing it because it needs external motivation"

What we really want from ourselves is a healthy body, mind and spirit. The only way to have these things is to control your mind. I wanted to go running but the urge to stay in bed was stronger, so I stayed in bed. Did I really get what I wanted, or did I take the easy way out? I don't think I need to answer this. Stay strong and own this afternoon of day three. Stop accepting and start achieving! Stop allowing outside forces to control you and start controlling yourself. It is a little awkward at first, but it is effective. Eric Thomas also says, "the lion doesn't need external motivation because he is driven by hunger", I'm paraphrasing but you get the idea.

7

A STORY FROM MY OWN DAY THREE

I wake up on day three and it's a whole different story than days one and two. I had a long day at work yesterday and I didn't sleep well last night, so I had no desire to get out of bed this morning. Getting started seemed almost impossible. I forced my feet to go to the floor, but my mind was fighting me the whole way. What are you doing? No one is making you get up this early so go back to sleep! I fought these urges by just taking the next step. I wasn't sure about the step after that, but I was determined to take the step directly in front of me.

As I stood up, another variable came into the equation. Every muscle from my chest to my toes started to scream at me. I was in some real pain, but I kept walking across the floor to the sink. As I finished brushing my teeth and getting dressed, I still wasn't sure if I was going to lay back down or walk out the door.

I somehow managed to force myself out the door and onto the street and began to run. I had the most motivating thing I could think of playing on my earbuds and I tried to ignore the pain. Every step seemed to make it worse. I assumed I would loosen up as I ran but it wasn't the case today. I suddenly felt a little angry at myself for allowing these urges and pain own me. I decided right there that even if I had to lay on my side and roll, I would finish today's run. I wasn't committed to the challenge at this point, but I had just taken an important step. I had committed to this day of my challenge.

As I ran, I realized that trying to block out the pain was doing nothing for me, so I decided to focus intently on it instead. I started breaking it down and dissecting it. Where exactly does it hurt the most? When I found it or at least found the right muscle group, I started asking myself if it was as bad as it seemed? Just how bad can something hurt? What about the rest of the population that has real pain right now, how do I compare to them? Somewhere out there is a person that is in much worse pain than I and that person is sucking it up and moving forward, so I will too.

A funny thing happened when I started focusing on my pain. It seemed to go away almost entirely. Now, I'm sure much of this was all in my head but in reality, the pain was all in my head to begin with. We feel pain in our heads, so it must be possible to control it, at least how we react to it. Either way, my pain faded, and I felt like I had learned a lesson that I could possibly apply to other pains and feelings in my life. I have had injuries in the past and I was able to control the pain, but I always assumed that was an adrenaline rush. In this case, I seemed to be able to control my pain, just by accepting it.

I kept running and finished the morning off strongly but when my timer went off, I was adamant about doing a few stretches and drinking plenty of water. No need to deal with soreness and cramps any more that necessary. I was happy with my decision to hold off for a week on increasing my duration. I may have challenged myself enough just like it is.

8

DAY FOUR

THE MORNING

On the morning of day four, expect a little better scenario than you woke up to on day three. Getting through day three is a huge deal and you should take a moment to be happy about it. On day four, the cravings subside even more, and the world is a little brighter place. You can probably let your friends and family know that it is safe to interact with you again. That's a joke but it is likely that you were in a somewhat bad mood before, don't beat yourself up about it. Instead, just let it go and move forward.

There will still be cravings that you will need to fight off on day four, but you have gotten pretty good at it by now. Now that you made it past day three, we can broaden our focus a little and begin to learn some things about ourselves while we complete our challenge. Remember the technique that you have used in the past few days because there are still challenging times ahead and this technique works.

One challenge that you will face, if you haven't already, is free time. It is easier to deal with your challenge when you are busy working and focused on other things, but the weekend has a whole new set of challenges. When our hands and heads are busy working, we are not thinking about what we are doing or not doing for our challenge. When we have a lot of free time, we tend to be affected more by our habits. I can remember back when I used to smoke (about eight years ago), it seemed like I would look down and have a cigarette in my hand and not even remember lighting it. Of course, I would smoke it anyway which is why it was such a bad habit for me. Just for a reference, I smoked for eighteen years and when I quit smoking, I was smoking almost three packs per day. That's about $700 per month at today's cost!

Turning our focus back to free time, try to plan your free time instead of waking up and doing whatever hits you first. I know the weekends are meant for a more relaxed schedule than the work week, but a little planning will go a long way towards you successfully making it through the weekend. Planning your weekend should be easy and stress free. If you are going to barbecue for family, just plan what time you will start and finish, the menu and guest list. Then move on to the next event and do the same for it. Writing this plan and others like it will not only make you more organized, it will expose the times when you will be vulnerable in your challenge. Knowing these vulnerable times will allow you to plan for them and fill those times with things that will help you through. Being more organized will make you an all around better person.

The last thing I will say about the morning of day four is this, You may still not be totally committed to this challenge but by now you can see the value and you are closer to committing. You are pretty sure you can finish this challenge even though you know there will be many challenges ahead. Your determination flame has grown a little stronger with the passing of day three and it should feel great. Take a couple minutes to take in that great feeling and then let it go. I ask you to feel it because that's the stuff winners are made from. I ask you to let it go because the job isn't done yet.

THE EVENING

The evening of day four and you have beaten the pain and urges of the morning. The wind is beginning to realize that you are serious about this challenge and you think you may just be able to see the light at the end of the tunnel. Now the mind starts to panic again and tell you that this is a silly challenge. What can you even get out of this? It's not like you won't go back to the old way after the challenge. The truth is, after the challenge is successfully completed, there may still be an occasional urge that will come along, but it will be easily overcame. It will be more of a small ripple in a pond than the tidal wave it is now. Don't let your instinct talk you out of committing. That panic is coming from a fear of success that is built into all of us.

We all have a fear of being great. What if I make it to great and can't keep it? What if my fears are exposed, does that make me a fraud? Worse yet, what if others follow my greatness and I let them down. These fears sound silly when you speak them out loud but in our heads they can be terrifying.

After the you beat the "it means nothing" battle with your mind, you can relax but don't let your guard down. The pain and urges will be back again. They may be a little weaker or they may be stronger, but they are not stronger than you. After all, you created them, so you will always win the battle, if you decide to.

Take some time on day four to write down some of the answers to the questions you had on day two. Are they the same answers you had when you answered them before? Compare the answers, if you have them, and pinpoint the differences.

Take time to measure your determination. As your flame grows hotter and brighter, are you becoming the person you wanted to be? If yes, then make a note of what you are doing right. If no, then you will need to make some changes, but you are still making positive progress. Make the changes and keep going.

By now, you are probably beginning to see that the thirty-day challenge is about more than starting a good habit or breaking a bad habit. It's about becoming a becoming the best version of yourself. I won't elaborate at this time, but I will say that when you start to see this, it is both frightening and fascinating at the same time. For now, just keep being strong and protect your flame.

9

A STORY FROM MY OWN DAY FOUR

On day four, I woke up ready to run and feeling pretty good. At this point in the challenge, I was pretty sure that I could finish this challenge, but I wasn't willing to bleed for it. I knew what commitment felt like because I had felt it yesterday. Yesterday I was committed to the day and that was great, but I wondered if I would feel that for the overall challenge. The end of the challenge is so far away at this point that it seems crazy to sign up for commitment. In the past, I have talked about a ten-mile run. I talked about how mile four is harder to finish than mile nine. The reason is that you know that the end is near on mile nine but mile four is still far away from the end. At this point in the challenge, mile four seems to stretch for about ten days! I decided to finish this day and see what happened next, but I was pretty sure I would be up and at it again tomorrow.

As I ran, I had very little pain and soreness and I was surprised by that. After yesterday's painful start, I assumed they would all start off like that. I had a great run and was able to turn my thoughts toward other things. This helped me get my mind right and set my day up right. The day seems to go better when you start it off with a nice run.

Truthfully, the day seems to go better even if you start it off with a terrible run but that's a story for another day.

10

DAY FIVE

THE MORNING

On the morning of day five, expect to wake up to the same urges and cravings as yesterday but they should be starting to weaken even more. It has been five days since you started this challenge and you are still going. You should take a moment to feel great about this. At this point, you are certain that you are stronger than the urges and pain and your confidence is growing. Your determination flame is growing as well, and it is important to keep feeding it with reasons that you should keep going and thoughts about how bad it feels to give up. Remember, pain is temporary but giving up is forever.

As day five takes its turn trying to make you quit, and the urges and pain begin to wake up and try to overtake you, remember that you are the owner of everything you feel. You may not decide if you have pain, but you own that pain and you decide how you are going to respond. You have come this far, and you are strong enough to overcome the urges and pain. Take a moment this morning to focus on the pain and urges. What is the desire in them that keeps calling you? What would it feel like to just slip up this once? The purpose of this exercise is to beat the cravings when you are not on your terms. For instance, say you go out and have a drink or two and the urges hit while your guard is down, do you think you will still win the battle? Maybe you will but feeling the urges and pain in this way, a little at a time will increase your chances. Only allow yourself these thoughts for a moment and then go over the questions and answers you have been working on.

Take advantage of this early morning energy and get some answers to those questions. Again, compare those answers to the previous answers you came up with. Notice any changes. Also notice any other questions that come to mind as you are reading your previous answers. Get answers to those questions as well and save for later.

I want to offer an idea for the day. As you defeat your struggles today, I want you to keep this thought in the back of your mind – Others are today where you were yesterday. What I mean by this is, yesterday your cravings and urges were much stronger, and it took a little more energy to deal with them, even more so the day before that. So, as you meet people that look unapproachable, assume they are in a harder part of a challenge and try to help them. Even if it's only a brief smile, it may help them make it through a tough moment. Maybe they are going through a moment similar to some that you have recently experienced.

It is a good possibility that the person in question is not doing a thirty-day self-challenge because only the elite few will challenge themselves out loud. The truth is that everyone else is working on a challenge too, they just choose not to realize it. Whether they realize it or not, it is important to help them if we can. So, approach the unapproachable and offer a little humor or kind words, it could be what helps them beat their challenge.

The Evening

On the evening of day five, it isn't so much about beating the pain and urges as it is managing fatigue. At this point you will need to be aware of the term "battle weary". Being battle weary comes from fighting for long periods and you have been fighting day and night for five days now. It's not time to relax or take a break but it is time to manage your energy. It is time to start applying the correct amount of energy for each episode. If an urge is terrible then you will need to spend a lot of energy on it but, if it is a mild pain, just spend a little energy. You will make it through either way, even if you spend an excessive amount of energy on everything you face, but managing it will keep you from being aggravated and give you something else to focus on and practice.

Another thing to start doing on day five is planning who you will spend your time with. Who will you spend free time with and who will you try to spend your work time with? Now that you have gained some control over your challenge, you will need to surround yourself with people that believe in you. People that believe in you will help you make it through, even when you don't believe in yourself. Chances are, you will have moments of doubt when you don't believe in yourself. These moments are easier to deal with when you are surrounded by people that believe in you.

A good way to determine who believes in you is to talk about your challenge. Tell people about it and where you are and see their reaction. If they call you an idiot, maybe they are not the best person to have influencing you. If they are supportive, keep them as possibilities. I'm not saying you can never see you're not so supportive friends, I'm saying that you need positive influences around you every day.

Before you end your day, remember to check in on your flame. Is it growing? Remember that that flame has a name. The name is determination and through determination comes everything you ever wanted. Anything you have ever wanted to be and any place you have ever wanted to go. Try to assess your flame every evening before you end your day.

11

A STORY FROM MY OWN DAY FIVE

Day five or my challenge was a little different than the other days have been. I woke up early and hit the pavement, as always but the night before, I had a little too much fun. I attended an event for my company and drinks were served, and then more drinks were served and so on. I wasn't feeling my best on day five and hangovers are my kryptonite!

I jumped out of bed and hit the street before I had time to focus on the fact that I wasn't feeling well. Once I was up and running, it was too late to even consider the possibility of not getting it done or even doing it poorly. The first mile of the run was terrible but after that, I started to sweat some of the bad decisions out and feel a little better. As I ran, I took a moment to think about which was worse, running with pain and severe soreness or running with a hangover. I never came to a definitive conclusion.

Something else started to happen on day five, I began to see myself finishing this challenge. I still wouldn't call it full commitment but the image of myself not finishing this was beginning to fade. I had run through pain, laziness and now a full-blown hangover. I only have twenty-five days left and even the bad days aren't that bad, if you look closely at them.

12

DAY SIX

THE MORNING

D ay six and practice is over, you are ready for the challenge today. For those of you that are giving up a bad habit, the last few days have been rough and for those of you that are starting a healthy habit, the days may be getting a little tougher but either way, we all have a hill to climb. The important thing is to know that the hill is climbable, and you have what it takes to make it.

If you are quitting a bad habit, then the urges and pain are more bearable than they were a few days ago and they will continue to improve as time goes by. It is not time to let your guard down, you must prepare yourself every day for temptations and always be ready to go to your mental stronghold when necessary. If you are implementing a healthy habit, it may have been a little tougher this morning to get started than it was when you began this challenge. The newness is wearing off and you still have a long way to go. Take a moment this morning to think about the feeling of quitting. Now, think of how it will feel to complete this challenge and be able to honestly know you did it. Fatigue is still a concern at this stage so you must assess yourself and continue to pay close attention to your energy levels. As the urges and pain occur, only spend the necessary amount of energy to overcome them.

At this stage in the challenge, the wind is starting to change directions. The negative comments you were getting before are turning to disbelief. Instead of people saying, "you can't do this", now they are starting to look at you like you are made of something different than them. You are cut from a different cloth. You were born with something that they weren't. The wind stops telling you that you can't do it because you are obviously doing it. Instead of trying to stop you from succeeding, the wind now starts protecting itself.

People will tell themselves all kinds of crazy things in order to protect themselves from a successful person. Why? Because if they admit that they can be successful too, then they only things that are stopping them are excuses and lack of effort. No one wants to be thought of as lazy or full of excuses but very few people are willing to put in the effort it takes to be successful at anything. Therefore, they talk about you like you are some miracle that has an unfair advantage. I've been told "but I'm not like you, I don't like to get up and run in the mornings". They assume I was born loving to wake up and hit the street. I've even had people use God as an excuse. They say, "God has blessed you" and while this may be true, they are using it as an excuse so that they don't have to feel bad for their lack of effort. My response is "God will bless you too, if you get off of the couch and work". Saying things like this allows them to be bad at life and not be accountable.

My question for you is this – are you a miracle? Or did you work for this? I already know the answer. You worked for this. You fought pain and urges that you were sure you couldn't defeat, and you won. You took the initiative to get started, you stuck it out through the toughest days, and you are still going. Know this, only a few people will take the initiative to get started, even fewer will put in the effort it takes to overcome the wind and even fewer will stick in there long enough to finish. So, let's ask the question again – Are you a Miracle? The answer is yes!

THE EVENING

On the evening of day six, you may be beginning to feel the fatigue I spoke about before. The feeling isn't terrible but after you defeat each craving, there may be a sigh afterwards. This simply means you are becoming battle weary. You become battle weary when you fight and fight and still have a long way to go. It's important to know that battle weary is a daily battle, meaning that just because you are worn out this evening and feel like you barely finished the fight, it doesn't mean you won't be full of energy tomorrow morning. Also, just because you spend every ounce of energy you have today, that doesn't mean you won't have a surplus of energy tomorrow. In fact, your tolerance will increase as you go along. As you fight yourself through the daily battles, you become a little stronger each day as the pain and urges get weaker.

Not only do you become stronger, but you are also gaining another advantage. You have weight with you and as you keep propelling the weight forward, you are gaining momentum. Momentum is a great thing because once you get enough of it built up, you can pick your feet up and coast without losing speed. This allows you to take short breaks and conserve even more energy. We can apply this newfound surplus of energy to other things.

Before you call it a day, let's take a minute to check in on that determination flame. By now, that flame should be growing at a slightly faster rate than when you started. What is causing that flame to grow? It's not only the challenge, look deeper. When you think about your flame, what do you imagine being able to do? If you were determined to do something, what would it be? What is in that flame that you would do, even if you didn't have to? With that mindset, look over your questions and answers again and make changes as you see fit. Think about what is next. What are we going to do tomorrow to make it better than today? Ash yourself, is there even a possibility that you won't complete day seven of your challenge? I for one fully expect and believe that you will be back here tomorrow, working on your challenge and feeding your flame. Why? Because you are a miracle!

13

A STORY FROM MY OWN DAY SIX

O n day six, I'm up and running. I felt great from the moment I opened my eyes. I felt so great that I kept running long after my timer went off. I wasn't intending to push myself, the run just felt so good that I didn't really want to stop.

On day six I noticed something else going on. It was somewhat of a "payoff" for all the hard work I was putting into this challenge. Even though it was a great feeling, it brought with it a somewhat scary feeling. As I arrived at morning meetings or just met with coworkers and clients, they would still be yawning and trying to wake up and there I was, looking like I had been out running and winning the day. Others were starting to ask questions like "why are you such a morning person?" and "why do you look so happy?". My answer – "because I am happy".

The scary part of it was that I was starting to like that feeling a little too much. I was starting to crave the "aliveness" in the morning.

Something else to note about my day six, I no longer doubted that I would finish this challenge. I did have a moment where I wondered if I stop when the challenge is over. It is a great feeling in the morning to feel like you already defeated the day. To paraphrase Mark Twain – "Eat a live frog in the morning and nothing else that happens to you that day will seem so bad". In other words, knock out the hard part first so that you can enjoy the rest of the day.

For me, day six was a great day. I started out feeling great, had a great run and then finished off the day strong by doing remodeling work and getting ahead of some projects. I felt great form the moment I opened my eyes until I closed them and fell asleep. I have to say that I have many great days but days like day six are rare. I took note of this day and if I close my eyes, I can still remember how great it was.

14

DAY SEVEN

THE MORNING

I t's day seven of your challenge and you are still going. You have fought your way through pain and urges for an entire week and you should be proud. Take a moment to be happy and enjoy this moment because it's a huge accomplishment. You can even focus in on the pain for a few seconds and enjoy what that feels like. You may be asking why you would enjoy pain and the reason is that you have earned this pain. You worked hard for this pain and it represents the success you are fighting for. While you are enjoying this moment, think back to day one and two and remember how hard those days were and how much easier it is now. Did the world change and make things easier? No way, so what changed and made it easier? The answer is you; you have gotten stronger. The pain and urges are the same, but you have changed, let that soak in and then imagine what else will be easier as you grow stronger.

Now that you have taken a moment to see how much better you are at controlling the pain and urges, you can continue your journey. Begin to look at those questions you have been answering and expanding and put some meaning to them. I want to add another question to your list and it may require a little time to answer. What are your dreams made of? Not the dreams that just happen when you sleep but the dreams that you visualize during your free time. If you could do anything in the world, what would it be? Remove failure from the equation completely and think about what you would do. Don't just say, I would be a billionaire, be specific and put some time and effort into this question.

This question will lead to many others so if you haven't been writing your questions and answers down, you may want to start. You will take your list and review it daily during this challenge. As you review, more questions will come, and you will add them to the list and find answers. Also, your answers will become more detailed and some of them will change completely. It's fine to change your mind, just hang onto your notes from each day, just in case you want to compare later.

A quick look back to our pain and urges. You are still in the middle of a war and you must not lose focus on your challenge. Take a moment to use the technique we learned earlier in this challenge whenever the you feel the urges and pain. Close your eyes and go back to that mental place where you went before. Focus on any noises you hear and then turn that noise into background noise to set the stage for a peaceful encounter. Dissect the pain and urges and remember that you own them. Remember that you will never become a victim to your own pain. When you have full control, open your eyes and sit for a moment. Feel that sense of self-control and make a mental impression of it. Save that impression for later when you have a tough moment.

The Afternoon

This afternoon, I'd like you to spend a few minutes feeling your urges and pain intentionally. Even if you aren't feeling any pain right now, take a moment and practice feeling it. Feel those urges and decide what power they have over you. Think again about what it would feel like to give up now, after all you have been through. Go back to the beginning and think about why you started this challenge. Remember the things that you heard from the wind, in the beginning. Remember why you didn't allow your flame to be blown out by the wind and know that your flame is stronger than ever.

I intend to add a few elements to your journey as we continue. You may be asking yourself, what is next after I finish this challenge? Do I just go back to the old me? I want you to work on a few things, using the questions and answers that you have been reading and changing that will help you continue to transform into the person you want to be. This technique can be used your entire life but much of this will become habit over time. If you practice long enough, it will become instinctive. As you begin to choose the instincts you want, the ones you don't want will fade.

Moving forward, start focusing on the new version of yourself. We have focused a lot on the old you and why you want to change, now it's time to look at the new you and measure how far you have come. Your list of questions and answers will be important to this part of our journey so keep working on them. I will refer you back to them as you continue.

Over the next few days, I want you to start prioritizing these questions and answers. Decide which ones are more important. What is the most important question? When you determine the most important question, assign a number one to it. Keep going and find the second most important question and give it a two. Keep doing this until you have numbered each question. When you are finished, you will know better where to spend your energy.

Focus most of your energy on the priority one question. When you get priority one completed, just move down the line in the same manner. When you have all the answers, hang on to them, we will be reviewing these daily, as mentioned earlier.

Before you close out the afternoon, check on your flame again. Is your flame getting stronger? Determination is the key element in this challenge, but it is much more than that. Determination is an important part of your life and from this point forward, it may be a focal point of everything you do. Could you see yourself giving up on your challenge, at this point? Would you be willing to give up now, even if you had a great excuse? We will never know because you are committed to this challenge and nothing will stop you.

15

A STORY FROM MY OWN DAY SEVEN

On day seven, I woke up feeling pretty good, until my feet hit the floor. My legs were not happy with the idea of going running again. I told myself that I would just jog slowly and take it easy, this at least allowed me to get started. Sometimes, it's easier to get started when we imagine a slow and easy task vs imaging ourselves out there killing it.

I hit the street and every muscle in my legs feels like it's being stabbed repeatedly. After a few minutes, my back muscles decided to chime in on the stabbing as well. I kept telling myself that the muscles would loosen up, but they only seemed to get worse. I considered walking for a few minutes but then decided that would be out of bounds for my challenge and thereby letting myself down.

At this point, my mind tried every trick in the book to get me to stop but I wouldn't allow it. The more my mind tried to protect me from pain, the harder and faster I ran. As I ran through the pain, I made up my mind that nothing would stop me from finishing this challenge. If I had to drag myself down the street on my knees, I would do it.

Day seven was important for me because I learned why I started this challenge. In the past, I had struggled to finish things. I would always finish, but only because it was a requirement, often I would finish weaker than I wanted to. As I ran today, I realized that it is a character flaw of mine. I decided that this flaw would end with this challenge. No longer will I finish on a level that I wasn't excited about. I can and will become the best finisher I know. No exceptions.

A quick note, on day seven, I announced to myself that I was committed to this challenge and when I did, many things became clear. All the answers to my questions seemed to be within my grasp. I found the real value in the thirty-day challenge on day seven.

DAY EIGHT

THE MORNING

O n the morning of day eight, it's time to again think about fatigue and the term battle weary. Take note of how are you feeling this morning? How did you feel when you fell asleep last night? Did you have anything left in you or were you completely exhausted? Did you finish everything you wanted to do yesterday, or did you have to roll a few things over to today? Do you often roll things over to the next day or even put them off indefinitely? If you do these things, it doesn't mean that you suck, it means that you are using one hundred percent of your capacity.

We only have so much capacity in a day, that's the bad news. We can increase our capacity in the same way we build muscle. Keep working out your capacity and it increases, it's that simple. If you are wondering why it seems like a bigger problem than it was before, it's because you have added many activities to your daily schedule. It takes energy to fight off pain and urges and it takes energy to deal with the wind. Even if you are only ignoring the wind, it still subtracts from you.

The world is a better place if we start off on the right foot so take a moment to use the technique you have been using to control your mind and deal with pain. Remember, turn the sounds around you into background noise and focus on what it would feel like to give in to the pain and urges. Remember that regretful feeling of defeat, knowing that you had more fight in you. Now turn your focus toward the future. What will it feel like when you have achieved this goal that you challenged yourself to accomplish? What will it feel like to have a plan for your future that will help guide you through the tough moments? When you have sat long enough, open your eyes and feel that self-control. It feels great, doesn't it?

As you continue your journey and make positive changes, you will see an increase in your capacity. Also, less and less energy will be used to fight off pain and urges, as time passes. This will allow you to turn that energy towards other things. Maybe you were struggling to keep up before you started this challenge, if so, adding the challenge only made the problem worse. If that's the case, then there are a few things you can do.

You can work on intentionally increasing your capacity, which is a great idea for everyone. There are many books, videos and consultants out there that can help you increase your capacity. You can also look at how you handle your daily activities. Are you a micro manager? Do you feel like you are the only one that can-do things right? If so, then maybe you can learn to delegate and teach someone else to do some of the things you do now. This takes energy but you are about to have some extra energy soon anyway. Instead of using it to do things yourself, use it to teach someone to help you. Maybe there are things that you are doing that aren't necessary. If after all of this you are still having to roll things over to the next day, make sure they are the low priority things. The best way to do this is to start off your day doing the important things and whatever is left over will be low priority.

It is important to create a surplus of capacity for yourself. One reason is that we all need a little free time. I'm all about planning and preparing for everything but I always try to plan a little time where I have nothing to do. During the work week, I shoot for an hour before work. That's my time and I don't like to be disturbed. If I am disturbed, I try to make up for it later in the morning. If I'm planning for the weekend, I will try to give myself a little more time. Example, if I know we are going out on Friday night to have drinks, I will schedule only the necessities for Saturday. I don't perform well with a hangover, so I plan for it.

Another reason to have extra capacity is to better yourself. If you spend all your time putting out fires, it makes self-improvement difficult. Extra capacity will give you time to do research, read books and just talk to others and learn. Remember, if you want to climb to the next rung on the ladder, you must be ready to take on that role.

Before you move on with your day, take a moment to feel any urges and pain that you may have. Also, read over your questions and answers, check to see if you still agree with your answers. Add any questions or notes that you have and then let it go for the day. We will come back to that this afternoon. Lastly, take a moment to check on your flame. Is it growing? Are you determined to finish this challenge as strongly as possible?

You may be wondering what these questions and answers have to do with your thirty-day challenge and that's a fair question. These prioritized questions will be used to create a list of goals which will keep you on track and help you grow intentionally instead of by accident. How can we start our day off by doing the important things if we don't have a plan? Growing intentionally is a much more efficient way to grow. Imagine if the only way to learn that fire is hot is by sticking your hand into it. That's a tough way to learn. Now imagine that you had to stick your hand into every fire you encountered to learn that it is hot. This example is extreme but that's the difference between having a plan and not having a plan.

The Afternoon

It's day eight and you have put the morning behind you. The pain and urges are still present, but you are certain that they have no power over you. In fact, you have power over them. You must decide to be affected by them in order to even feel them. You are aware that they could come back strong and at weak moments but right now, on day eight, they are nothing.

As you start off the evening on day eight, take a moment to think about what you really want. Instead of thinking and writing down multiple questions and answers, I want you to focus on the priority one question. Now, think about that one thing for a minute. Does this thing motivate you? Is it something that you can achieve easily? If it's easy, then go get a new thing because we want something to strive for. Eric Thomas says, "if it's easy, it ain't worth nothing" and I agree with him.

Now let's take that one thing and determine what you must do to get there. Think about how to turn that question into a goal and what you need to achieve that goal. Do you need more money than you currently make? Do you need family to help you with it? What is the first step you would have to take to reach that thing? I want you to ask yourself these questions in order to find out what you should be doing, in order to reach what you want.

Now that we know what the first step is, why not take it? I'm not telling you to quit your job or jump off a bridge but if it takes more money than you currently make to get there then how do you get it? Can you make more money at your current job? Maybe there are other options for you? Could you take on a side job or project. Maybe money has nothing to do with it.

If money is not the problem, then address the other issues. Do you need buy-in from you family in order to get it? If so, then take the time to research, plan and come up with a way to pitch it to them. A way that you know they won't refuse. Don't just walk up and say, I think we should do this, and I need your help. Have the details laid out and know who will perform what tasks, how it will be done and why.

Whatever it is that you need in order to take that next step, take the time to get it moving. On day eight, I want you to learn how to do things that will suit you. Don't follow your neighbor because he is successful, and you aren't yet. Go after what you want and don't let the wind stop you. You can talk to successful people and use them as mentors but only follow them if they are going the same way as you. If others don't believe in your path, its because it is your path and not theirs, they aren't required to believe in it. Don't let opinions stand between you and your goals.

Now look at those prioritized questions and answers again. Start by reviewing and making sure you still agree with everything. Next, rewrite them or type them, whatever you choose. When you rewrite them, write them in the form of a goal, the same as you did for the priority one question you focused on earlier. Now keep the number you used to prioritize them and add a letter below each question. If you have more than one answer, then use the letter b. and then c. and so on. Do this for all of them and then put it away.

Before you call it a night, check back in on your flame. Take a moment to compare it to the flame you started with. Look at the differences and remember how fragile it was. Is there a chance that the wind could blow this flame out? Maybe but it would take them a long time and you would have to allow them time and access. Champions don't allow others to blow out their flame and you are a champion.

17

A STORY FROM MY OWN DAY EIGHT

O n day eight, I woke up to a sore body, but I paid little attention to it. I did a few stretches and then hit the street. I wanted to write that it was tough at first, but it turned out that it was tough the entire run. It's a good thing that I found my commitment yesterday!

As I ran through the pain on day eight, I assumed that I would just get sorer and slower until I reached day thirty. I had a vision in my mind of me crawling down the street for the last week of the challenge. I knew that was a little dramatic, but I decided that I would do that, if that's what it came to. Death was the only thing that would stop me from completing this challenge. I didn't share this with anyone at the time, but I promised myself that nothing would keep me from a strong finish.

As I ran on day eight, I learned that pain is unable to stop me from doing what I want to do. Pain is not a showstopper. Pain can even become irrelevant if you are determined enough. I will even go as far as saying that we can begin to crave pain in some cases. When we go to the gym or workout, we crave the soreness, because the reward is in the soreness. We don't skip workouts because we feel a little pain.

I also had time to think about how this pertains to the mental side of us. We can overcome and use mental pain as well. If you have never mentally pushed yourself to the point where your head is throbbing and your eyes feel like they will explode then you may not understand but for those of us that do this often, you know what I mean. In short, I will say that are driven or at least a little bit addicted to the grind. We crave mental and physical soreness because it represents growth.

18

DAY NINE

THE MORNING

O n the morning of day nine, you wake up, beat the cravings and then check your fatigue level. You have become pretty good at beating the cravings and urges and your determination flame is becoming a fire. Others are starting to see and feel this fire. They know there is something different about you but they don't know the details.

The people that are closest to you already know the details and they are amazed. Some of them won't admit it and others will tell you how proud they are. At the beginning of this challenge, I told you to guard your flame from the wind to keep it from being blown out. While this is still true, a little positive wind can fan the flames and help you grow. The best way to receive positive wind is by helping others.

As others watch you grow stronger, they will begin to follow you. While it is a great thing, it comes with responsibilities. When people are following you, it's extremely important to lead them with their best interest in mind. Never lead people just because you want something from them. You must lead as a servant.

Before you can effectively lead others, you will need to really see yourself for what you are. I don't mean looking in the mirror, I mean what kind of person are you? The answer to this question will be forever changing because you are forever growing but you need to know where you are right now. It is difficult for people to see the real person that they are, unless they look hard for it.

What we vision in our heads is often nothing like we truly are. The way to see the real you is to first, self-assess. Ask yourself how you feel about leading others. If the follow me, can I lead them to a great place? Am I willing to do what it takes to keep them safe along the road? Am I willing to learn in order to be a better leader? There are many books and blogs about leadership that will help you along the way, if you are willing to be a leader.

The second thing to do is, find out how others see you. Do they see you as the person you want them to see you as? Ask them the same questions you would ask yourself and see if it aligns with what you think is best for them. Remember, at this point, you are trying to see where you stand today. When the time comes, you will decide if you want to lead others or if you want to walk alone. You have already proven that you aren't a follower by breaking the cycle and improving yourself. Keep in mind that helping and leading others is one of the best things you can do for yourself. In reality, the only things we get to keep forever are the things we give away.

Getting back to today, let's review those questions and see how they stack up to your heart today. Are the answers still correct? Are the questions still relevant? Add any other questions you have and answer them. Be sure to keep the same format we used before.

Now, before we get away form the morning, look back at that flame. Now keep the flame in mind and think about leading others. Don't even consider failure as an option right now. Just think of the flame and leading others to a successful place. Does your flame intensify? Now ask yourself again if you want to be a leader or walk alone. There is no wrong answer and you aren't required to keep the same answer forever.

The Afternoon

As the afternoon arrives, go ahead and defeat those cravings and urges, as you have been doing for the last nine days. After you defeat them, take a moment to be happy about where you are now. Feel that commitment you made to this challenge and enjoy it for a second. It is like looking into the future because you know you will finish this. The wind is hardly a factor at this point, unless it is a positive wind.

Going back to helping others, even if you decided to walk alone, you can and should still help others. Not only can you help others through a bad time but you can also learn from them. Helping others is one of the fastest ways to grow. That's not the reason you should help others but it is definitely a benefit. The best way to help others is to be there for them.

Sometimes people will come to you because they see you as a strong person. They think that you must be a strong person because you set goals and you accomplish them. Again, you are a miracle in the eyes of others. We must be cautious not to try to fix people. Our first helpful instinct is often to troubleshoot and solve the problem but that is usually a bad idea. When someone comes to you, they often just want to be heard by a strong person. Take the time to listen and reassure them that they have what it takes. Don't start offering solutions. Offering solutions leads to trouble for both of you.

As you wind down your day today, take a moment to be happy about your progress. You have made it through much in the last nine days and you deserve it. At this point in you challenge, you will stop "making it through" and start doing it because you want to do it. The cravings and urges will still be there and your mind will question you and try to cause doubt but you will crush them immediately. You don't have time for cravings or self-doubt because you have people to help in this world.

The last thing I want you to do today is to go back to your flame. Take a look at it and ask yourself if it has grown today. I bet it has, in fact, I bet you are amazed at the size of your determination vs when we first started. Remember, everything you have ever wanted, is in that flame, all you have to do is get it.

19

A STORY FROM MY OWN DAY NINE

D ay nine and I'm on the street running at five am. I'm still hurting but not as bad as the last couple days. I'm actually enjoying the soreness and it seem almost pleasant. I had another late evening with a few adult beverages but I hardly even notice it today.

Today, the pain is so slight and easy that I am able to focus on some of the daily challenges that I face. As I ran, I began to compare what I'm doing to other activities and I find that there are many similarities. This challenge has been a rollercoaster ride so far, with many ups and downs. Some days have been the best ever and others I felt lucky to survive them.

I took a moment to assess my flame. I noticed that there is a bonfire of determination for this challenge. I then compare my flame for this challenge to other areas in my life, other things that I'm committed to and I find some determination there but maybe not the bonfire I was looking for. As I said before, this challenge was about me being a better finisher so I will keep an eye out for improvement.

When I started this challenge, I knew it was about more than just running and on day nine, I made a connection between the challenge and my everyday commitments. I began to wonder if other things would work in my daily life. When I'm in pain, can I focus on it and make it subside? Can I strengthen my weaknesses? I think we both know that the answer is yes.

20

DAY TEN

THE MORNING

S o here we are, the morning of day ten and we are about to put one third of this challenge behind us. It's not even half way over and I'm starting to miss it already! Take a moment this morning to feel one of your cravings. Really take it in and see what it feels like. Does it have any power over you? Is there any chance that you would give in to it at this time? Of course not, because you own the cravings and you are the decision maker. Now that we have our cravings and urges where we want them, we can move on the other things. Let's start off with thinking like a successful person.

Successful people have a way of thinking that protects them from the wind, gossip and other negative environmental conditions. You will have a hard time catching a successful person standing around gossiping about other people. It is also very rare to see a successful person that is telling someone that they can't do it. The successful person will never project their own insecurities onto others. Instead, they are positive all of the time. If they have a negative moment, and we all do, they protect others from it. If a successful person see a weakness in you, they will find a way to speak to you about it and help you strengthen it. That's the right thing to do and that's what successful people do. When someone tries to project negativity onto a successful person, they immediately see the weakness in that person and try to help them. They do it because they want to help, not because they have something to gain.

Another thing that successful people do is they fail. Successful people fail often and they fail hard. They fail often because they try often. They don't play it safe and only try things that they are pretty sure will work out. They see what they want to do and they go for it. They fail hard because they are giving it everything they have. They don't care that others are watching and will see them fail. They give it everything because the only acceptable fear is the fear of not trying hard enough.

This morning as you are reviewing your questions, look at them from the perspective of a successful person. If some of the questions aren't in line with the successful you then what do you need to do to fix them. Do you need better answers? If so, then give yourself a better answer. Take a look back to your first set of questions and answers and see if any of them seem silly now. If they do seem silly, it's because you have grown past that level. Do this often to see your growth pattern and make a note of how you have grown.

Now, before we end the morning, let's take a quick look at that flame. Is it time to start referring to it as a fire yet? I bet it is. Your determination has grown to new levels and the fact that there is no chance of not finishing this thirty day challenge confirms that. Not only has your flame grown but you have been feeding it the right fuel. You are reading about successful people and ways to be successful. That's also what successful people do. They read books that keep their skills sharp and help keep them motivated. The books may be something they have already learned but they are still motivating. They may have even read the same book before and liked how it made them feel. Keep reading and feeding your fire, you are doing great.

The Afternoon

Here we are on the evening of day ten, about to put a full ten days behind us and you are still making it happen. Take a moment to enjoy the passing of the first third of your challenge. You have made it a full third of the way and that's something to smile about. Think back to day one and remember how much of a struggle it was and how much easier it is now. We have come a long ways. For those of you that are quitting something, it's becoming easier every day. For those of you that are implementing a new habit, it has been getting a little harder each passing day but it will level off soon. Either way, keep your head up and be happy that you have made it this far because most people that started with you quit long ago. Most of them on day one or two. Many of the people that are using this book to guide them will also fail but remember what successful people do. They fail often and hard.

I want you to focus on your questions again this afternoon. Review them and your answers. Now that your questions and answers are fresh in your mind, let's add another layer to the list. Last time we rewrote the list we used a number for each question and a letter for each answer. Now I want to add a small dot under each answer and write in the steps it would take to achieve that answer. If there are no steps and it's a simple answer then write what you can gain from the answer.

When you finish, it should look something like the figure on page 43. By now, most of you have determined that this challenge is about much more than just a challenge. You have also noticed that we are beginning to form an outline with these questions. For now, we will use this outline to review and make sure we are happy with our questions and answers. We will review these often and when we have grown enough to be sure we are happy with these questions and answers, we will put this outline to good use.

1. Question
2. Answer number one

- Step
- Step

1. Answer number two

- Step
- Step

1. Question   .
2. Answer number one

ONCE YOU HAVE FINISHED YOUR QUESTION AND ANSWER outline, let's take a look at that flame again. Do you notice that the flame tends to fluctuate? When we are pumped up and motivated, it is a raging fire and when we are busy writing questions and answers outlines, it seems to die down a little. It is important to pay attention to these changes and understand them. We will talk more about these changes later but for now, start noticing what makes your flame burn hotter. Write it on the bottom of your outline each day so we won't forget. As you call it a night, see yourself as that successful person and conduct yourself accordingly.

21

A STORY FORM MY OWN DAY TEN

I t's day ten and I'm not feeling great but I'm also not in constant pain. My desire to finish this challenge is still growing and I'm already thinking about the next challenge. There are so many things about myself that I want to change and I want to continue improving myself at the art of finishing. This challenge is a physical challenge and I'm inclined to challenge myself academically for my next challenge.

I wonder if it's too early to be thinking about the next challenge since I'm only on day ten of the current challenge. After some thought, I decide that I can start thinking about the next challenge, I can even make a decision and get started but I must be committed to it as well.

As I run, I think about this challenge and I decide that it may have been a little self-centered or even greedy. This was all about improving myself and if I look at my own writings, helping others is more rewarding. The truth here is that I must do both. There is an old saying "you can't pour from an empty cup", which means I have to keep improving myself, if I want to improve others. The greedy part is that I'm the only person that gets to feel the aliveness and accomplishment after my morning run and I really would like to share it.

How great would it be if I could do a thirty day challenge that benefitted others. If I could do something academic and have the ability to share it with others that want to improve, that would be a great thing. Not only would this benefit others but it also offers certain values to myself. This challenge is running at five am, I would hardly consider this public. It is dark and I'm pretty much hidden from the world. Most people are still waking up and getting dressed so there are very few eyes on me, as I run. To complete a challenge that the public could see would be a challenge all by itself for me.

DAY ELEVEN

THE MORNING

It's day eleven and you have lived to fight another day. Your cravings come back at you this morning but you easily over power them and move on. You aren't spending any more energy than you need to on the cravings so your fatigue is in check. You should be feeling pretty good right about now. Things are beginning to happen like you want them to and it feels great. Other People are starting to believe in you as well. They are watching you easily defeat your cravings and urges and again, they think you must be made of something different than them. They have already forgotten about the first couple of days when the urges and cravings were strong. If your challenge is to do something for thirty days then they are waiting to see if you will keep going.

As I said before, it is okay to enjoy the positive wind when you hear it but don't get caught up in it. Also, don't let the negative wind affect you in any way. Dealing with negativity in any form takes energy and we are still being cautious with our energy. The only good reason to deal with negativity is if you are helping someone. And even then, you cannot let it get to you. If you notice yourself being affected, you will need to find a new approach.

Now that we have talked about others, let's talk about you. I want you to be honest with yourself and pick apart your own weaknesses. What affects you in a negative way? What do you do that would negatively affect others and/or their situations? How do you respond to others when they are negative? Do you join in? Do you react harshly? One of my weaknesses that I wanted to improve with my first challenge was finishing. If you remember, I talked about it previously.

As you go about your normal day, take a look at the things you excel at but also pay close attention to the things you would like to change about yourself. It is important to detect and write these weaknesses down. We will have a need for these later but for now, just capture every weakness you see. If you think it needs to be improved, write it down. Don't let yourself get away with things like "Everyone is bad at dealing with changes" or "I finish as strong as anyone else that I know". This isn't about others, this is about you. We want to be as good as we can be not as good as we feel we need to be.

Before you get away from the book this morning, take a look at that flame. How is it looking? It should be burning bright this morning because you have come so far and dealt with so much and you are still going. Not only are you still going but you are actually improving and gaining momentum. I said earlier that "others are starting to see the change in you" but the reason is because you are starting to see the change in you. Keep your head up and know that you deserve to see yourself in a new way.

The Afternoon

As the afternoon rolls in and you prepare for the cravings and urges that will try again to keep you from being successful, take a moment to feel those cravings. Pick them apart and ask yourself, just what are they trying to tell you? Are they offering you anything that will make you great? Now that you aren't susceptible to these cravings and urges, it's important to study them and determine what they are made of. Doing this will only make you stronger for future challenges. And believe me, there will be other challenges.

Of course, life will throw challenges at you all the time and you will receive challenges from co-workers and family but there will also be many more self-challenges. When you walk away from this challenge and see how much better you have made yourself, you will want to do the thirty-day self-challenge for everything. And you will find that it works every time.

Comparing yourself to others is never a good thing but learning from others is a great thing. Pay attention to coworkers and friends and family as you go through your day. Look for things they do that you admire, don't try to pick apart their routines and habits but try to absorb their qualities. You may find a way to strengthen one of your weaknesses. If you know the person well enough, you may want to ask them to elaborate on a strength of theirs but don't comment on any weaknesses that you think you see. Remember, today is about fixing you, not them. I find that the world is a happier place when others bring their weaknesses to you. There are exception to this but it's a good general rule. If you see someone that could get hurt, you may want to have a conversation with them. Also, if they are doing something that is considerably affecting them negatively, it may be an exception. Always put yourself in their shoes and approach them in the way you would want to be approached.

Now, let's take another look at your own weaknesses. What did you learn today? Did you find plenty of things that need improvement? I want you to write each weakness down that you found and put the number one beside each weakness. Then I want you to write a way to improve that weakness below it using the letter a. Continue this for each weakness. Put some thought into these improvements. Ask yourself why is it a weakness? How much energy will it take to improve it? What will happen if I don't improve it? What will happen if I do improve it? Any other questions or notes that you can think of for each weakness is helpful so write those down too.

The next thing to do is to prioritize these weaknesses and improvements. Start with the weakness that negatively affects you the most and use it as number one. Then take the most likely improvement process and use it for letter a. Continue this for each weakness and then we have another outline started. We will stop at this step for the afternoon but feel free to read over it and be creative as much as you like.

Before you call it a day, take an assessment of your flame and see how it is growing. Remember to expect some fluctuation but we want to see a slight upward trend. Your determination is the key to your success so, it's important that your flame keeps growing. One way to keep it growing is to keep fueling it with things that will positively affect you and another way is to fuel it with passion. Both of these things are important and we will talk more about them in the near future.

23

A STORY FROM MY OWN DAY ELEVEN

D ay Eleven, it's five am and I'm up and running. I have very little pain this morning and I'm feeling the need to succeed. I am running at a much faster pace than I did the last few days and this adds fuel to my fire. With the absence of pain, I'm able to allow my mind to drift and focus on other things. This allows me to accomplish my challenge and clear my head at the same time. It is a huge time saver.

I'm feeling a little pressure at my job so this becomes my first focus point. I've been asked to assess the overall financial situation of a small company so my focus has been directed at others. While this is my job and I'm good at it, there is always a toll to pay when you are grading others. As I run, I turn the inspection flashlight on myself and I find a few things that I want to improve immediately. I send myself an email, which isn't easy when running but I manage, so that I don't forget what these things are.

I turn my focus back to the run and I'm surprised to see that it's almost finished. I try not to focus on any deep thoughts for the rest of the run, instead I pay attention to my surrounding environment. I notice the trees and the ditched and creeks and even the places where it is pitch black from darkness. In the past, I never really gave much thought to the phrase "be in the moment" but this morning, I began to understand. As I honed in on my surroundings, I felt things that I didn't realize I could feel. As I passed over the creek, I could feel a slight temperature change. I removed my headphones and listened to the sounds as I ran. I was amazed at how many different sounds there were. I decided that there may be some value to "being in the moment".

Later in the day, I gave it a try again. In the world we live in today, we multitask everything. Even the things that don't require it. How many times have you sat down, turned on the television and then grabbed your phone. Unless something pulls you away from the phone, you don't even really watch the tv. We eat and watch tv and play on the phone. I realize it's a time saver but try eating all by itself. What I learned is that conversation is better, food has more flavor and there is a feeling of satisfaction that you get when you are "in the moment"

24

DAY TWELVE

THE MORNING

It's day twelve and you have put eleven days of this challenge behind you. This morning, I want you to take a few minutes to think about how you feel about your challenge so far. Does it feel great? Or does it feel like an obligation? Are you looking at it from an opportunity point of view or are you seeing it as a chore? When you feel the pain, do you wish it would go away or do you face that pain and pull it apart? I ask these questions because I think it's time that we start enjoying ourselves as this challenge progresses.

If you feel like you must force yourself to make every move we are making, you will still finish this challenge but I want you to do more than just finish this challenge. I want you to change your life and be a better version of you. In order to do this, we need to enjoy the rest of this challenge. Your cravings and urges are easily defeated at this point, so you aren't suffering. We are doing some activities that aren't exactly fun but if you really get into it and become engaged, you will enjoy it. If you have any resistance, I ask you to let it go at this point and trust yourself. Put real thought into your questions and weaknesses as you review them and re-write them. Listen to your heart and ignore the doubtful mind.

Now let's focus on your questions outline. Review it and make changes as you need to. Are your answers still the same? Are there better questions that you want answers to? Do these questions and answers have an effect on you? If so, then what is the affect? Is it positive or negative? Are the questions still prioritized correctly? Are the steps still relevant and correct?

Now let's go over those weaknesses again. Do you feel like these are your only weaknesses? Do they still feel relevant? Think about what it would mean if you were to strengthen each one of these weaknesses. How would that feel? Would you be as strong as you can possibly be? Take a look at your answers. Are they still correct? Are you moved when you read over your answers or does it feel rushed or weak? Now is the time to add, change and rewrite, if necessary. Remember, all of these will be forever changing so there is no need to be rigid. At this point, we are going through the changing mind and trying to break through the first draft. Once we have reviewed it enough, we will finish our outline and turn that into a plan. A plan that will help you know what to do for each passing second of the day. You won't need this plan for your everyday activities but when you stall out, you will have something that will get you moving again. Your very own personal motivational book.

I want to share a brief moment with you and talk about my reasoning for reviewing as much as we have. Often, we have questions and/or ideas that are good enough to remember. They seem great when we think about them but the next day, they seem less great. A little later they seem like a totally useless idea and we move on from it. I want to make sure your questions, answers and weaknesses are truly what you want to focus on before we nail it down. That's my reasoning behind reviewing daily and nightly for a few days. At the beginning of this challenge, it also gave us something other than the cravings, urges and pain to focus on, so it was a win-win.

Before we move on from the morning, let's take a quick look at that flame and see how it looks. Has it grown even more? When you think about the changes you are making, does it seem to burn even hotter? Are you feeding your flame the correct information? We are looking for a balance between your questions, your weaknesses and your flame, does it feel like we are improving everything at the same pace? If not, where are we lacking. Pay a little more attention to that area until we are balanced.

The afternoon

It's the afternoon of day twelve and you have put another morning behind you. What will we do with the rest of your day? I would like you to take something you consider hard and do it for a while this evening. Before you decide that you are just going to suck it up and do it, I want to try it a little different. The thing you choose can be anything you consider hard but are capable of doing. If you are physically capable of running but hate doing it, try that. If you find writing hard, try writing. Write anything, as long as you find it to be something hard.

Before we starting doing the difficult thing, Let's take a moment and think about it. If it's running, how long will we run? How fast will we run? Should we take a moment to walk a little before we run or just get it out of the way? Maybe if we take a few really deep breaths before we start, we will be able to control our breathing better? What is the most important thing to control as we run? Now that you have thought it over and made decisions, let's begin.

I'm going to use running for my example but the thought process is the same. As you begin running, take those deep breaths and choose your pace. Forget about everything else except the choices you made before you started. Before you let your mind decide that this sucks, take a moment to feel it. Is it really that bad? If you don't try to hate it, could you even enjoy it a little?

I asked you to do this exercise for a couple of reasons. One reason is to see how much of a difference it makes when we create a plan, open our minds and execute our plan. If you had just jumped up and ran, you may have hated it as always. The second reason is to feel that upstream battle. Everything worthwhile is upstream so it takes a lot of effort. We won't always like what we have to do but if we plan, open our minds and execute, we may find a way to enjoy it. Simply put, the right way and the hard way are often the same way. So get used to dealing with the hard way. Its important to know that as we do the hard thing more and more often, it becomes less and less hard.

Now, back to our outlines, let's review our information one last time as the day closes. Read your questions and ensure they are prioritized correctly. Then read your answers and each step you have listed to make sure you are satisfied with them. After that, read over your weaknesses and ensure that they are also correctly prioritized. Then check you solutions and finally add the steps under your solutions. I refer you back to the table on page 43 for a reference. No sense in changing our format. Let's keep it uniform.

When you finish with your review, take a look at your fire and see how your determination is growing. Are we working on the things that mean the most to you? If not, you will need to review and edit your outlines again. If we are then you should be building some determination. Pay attention to your flame often because it is directly linked to your passion. If you find your flame dying down, you may be heading down a path that you don't have passion for. In that case, you will need to make some changes.

A STORY FROM MY OWN DAY TWELVE

As I start to run on day twelve, the pain returns and I'm not even unhappy about it. I'm even a little excited to have the pain back. The pain seems to break up the monotony of doing the same thing every day. Since I have the pain to focus on, I don't really need to dive deep into my own mind so it's somewhat of a break.

About five minutes into my run and it starts to rain. Slowly at first and then it turns into a real downpour. I considered stopping my run for a moment. I could just do it later or I could use the heavy rain as a great excuse, anyone with a brain would be headed for shelter right now. See how those cravings and urges wait for a weak moment and try to break in? Anyway, I am determined to finish this run right now. No amount of rain or bad weather will stop me and I refuse to break my challenge.

Running in the rain at five am in pain may not sound like much fun but it really wasn't that bad. As I ran, a few cars passed by me and for a brief moment, I felt embarrassed. They probably think I'm crazy, out here running in the pouring down rain but I quickly dismiss this type of thinking. I decide to focus on what is getting done instead of what others think. What really counts is the original goal. The goal of being a great finisher and this day twelve proves my commitment to the goal. The truth is that I felt exhilarated while I was running in the rain. If you are out running at five am on a dry day and it feels lonely, you should try it on a day when its pouring down rain!

DAY THIRTEEN

THE MORNING

Its day thirteen and you are quickly approaching the half way mark. Remember that story about how mile four is harder than mile nine on a ten mile run? Well we are about to finally finish the metaphoric mile four. If you have any cravings that are out of the ordinary this morning, close your eyes and deal with them accordingly. Take time to pick those cravings apart and feel them for a moment. If there is pain, feel it. Pinpoint that pain and figure out what makes it tick. Why is it allowed to affect you so much? Can I control it? If I can't control it, can I handle it? Remember what Eric Thomas says "if it's easy, it ain't worth nothing". Also, remember this, stay focused longer than others. In a competitive situation, this will always give you an edge and right now you are competing against the old you.

After you have controlled your mind, take a look at your mental self and see what your condition is. Are you fatigued? How is your attitude? Do you feel coachable? I know that going over these outlines gets to be monotonous but it's an important part of the future. The truth is that even if you never touch the outlines again, you will still succeed at this challenge. You will still live and survive as you always have but do you really want to look back from your death bed and say "I survived" or "I existed"? I don't and if it means working on these outlines and finding a way to be excited about it then that is what I will do. I know you will too because you are still going after all you have been through during this challenge.

After you have yourself in a coachable mood, let's take a look at those outlines. Start with the questions and answers. Are the questions starting to form a path forward towards your desires and goals? We started with questions about your determination and how your flame was growing, now we need to ensure that we are growing in the right direction. Your questions should be changing into questions about how to grow that flame, improve your life and what it will do to help the others that are around you.

Let's move on to your weaknesses, are the weaknesses still relevant? Are your solutions solid? What about your steps that you recently added, do they still make sense? Are you adding any weaknesses? Do you find yourself doing little things during the day that will help strengthen some of your weaknesses? As you go through your weaknesses, ensure the priority in in the correct order.

As you go through your day today, I want you to again take notice of others. See them as they are instead of what they are trying to project. Also, try not to form an opinion before you speak to them for a few minutes. I can see someone across the room and form an opinion of what that person's attitude is. There is no reasoning behind this, it's just human nature to assume that someone is mean, if they look mean. I see myself as the most approachable person in the world. If I catch you looking at me, I will notice you and give you a smile. Others tell me that I'm six feet four inches tall, bald headed and I look like I want to harm them. While I am a big bald guy and I often look like I'm serious, I only intend to help others, not harm them. Try to speak to the person before you assume something about them. If you get the opportunity to help someone today, help them.

THE AFTERNOON

On the afternoon of day thirteen, I want to recap what you found while noticing others. Did you find people that looked mean but were actually nice? Or did you find that most people are exactly like you assumed they would be? I find that there are often both of these situations. I don't judge people by their expression and I always try to speak before forming an opinion. This has saved me from putting a label on people and regretting it later. Were you able to help someone today?

This afternoon, I will only ask you to read over your outlines briefly. As you read over them, ask yourself this question, Are they excellent? Or do they just seem like words on paper. If they are excellent then they are keepers but if they are just words, we still have work to do. Its likely that they aren't excellent so if they aren't then be thinking about what will make them excellent. I am not the judge here, only you can decide what excellence is for you. Successful people desire and require excellence. Both from themselves and others.

As you finish off your evening, take a look at your flame of determination and see what it is doing. Think about your outlines and see how it reacts. Does it flare up when you think about what lies ahead? What about your current career, does it flare up when you think about it? If it does then great but if it doesn't, we need to find out why. What part of your career makes it flare up? What part makes it die down? Maybe there is no part that makes it flare up, why doesn't it? I say again that your flame is directly linked to your passion. While you may need a job to pay your bills, you should also be always seeking your passion. If your passion is totally different than your current path then be thinking of how you will correct it.

A Story From My Own Day Thirteen

Day thirteen and I'm running with very little pain. I got a late start and it's right at the edge of daybreak. I've been running in the dark for so long that I almost feel a little exposed as I run. Since I have on pain to focus on today, It leaves me no choice but to do some thinking during my run.

I start off with some deep thought about my work. Some people will say that you should leave work at work but I believe that only applies if you hate your work. In my case, I love what I do so I think about it as much as possible. If you really do hate your work, your number one priority aside from starving, should be finding a way to work on something different. I would hate to know that I had to work at something that I hated for my entire life.

I turn my thoughts to life in general and start recapping some of the decisions I've made recently. Did I make the right decisions? Should I have done more research before making the decisions? You probably think I'm doubting myself with these questions but this is what I call "reflection". I always like to reflect back and determine what I could have done better.

Reflection is an important part of our routines so if you aren't doing it, you may want to give it a shot. If you aren't growing at the pace you want, I would tell you to reflect more often. Take time to analyze your activities at least on a weekly basis.

Some people like to find a quiet place at home to reflect, others like to do it with the television playing in the background. Personally, I like to reflect while I'm running, cleaning house or working on a project. It seems to save me a little time by killing two birds with one stone. I realize that this contradicts what I recently learned about "being in the moment". I may have to change my game up and see what the quality difference is.

On day thirteen, I was able to reflect, capture and learn from the mistakes or choices I have made in recent times. Mistakes and failures are valuable, if we take time to learn from them.

27

A STORY FROM MY OWN DAY THIRTEEN

Day thirteen and I'm running with very little pain. I got a late start and it's right at the edge of daybreak. I've been running in the dark for so long that I almost feel a little exposed as I run. Since I have on pain to focus on today, It leaves me no choice but to do some thinking during my run.

I start off with some deep thought about my work. Some people will say that you should leave work at work but I believe that only applies if you hate your work. In my case, I love what I do so I think about it as much as possible. If you really do hate your work, your number one priority aside from starving, should be finding a way to work on something different. I would hate to know that I had to work at something that I hated for my entire life.

I turn my thoughts to life in general and start recapping some of the decisions I've made recently. Did I make the right decisions? Should I have done more research before making the decisions? You probably think I'm doubting myself with these questions but this is what I call "reflection". I always like to reflect back and determine what I could have done better.

Reflection is an important part of our routines so if you aren't doing it, you may want to give it a shot. If you aren't growing at the pace you want, I would tell you to reflect more often. Take time to analyze your activities at least on a weekly basis.

Some people like to find a quiet place at home to reflect, others like to do it with the television playing in the background. Personally, I like to reflect while I'm running, cleaning house or working on a project. It seems to save me a little time by killing two birds with one stone. I realize that this contradicts what I recently learned about "being in the moment". I may have to change my game up and see what the quality difference is.

On day thirteen, I was able to reflect, capture and learn from the mistakes or choices I have made in recent times. Mistakes and failures are valuable, if we take time to learn from them.

28

DAY FOURTEEN

THE MORNING

Day fourteen and here we are still going. It's half way eve, if you want to measure it. You are at the edge of a mile stone and you should be happy about that. Take a moment to compare how you feel now to when we first started. Make a mental note of the differences. It's pretty easy to defeat the cravings and urges as they try to attack you. Even if you are caught off guard by a craving, it's easier to get to that place where you can think it over. The place where noise turns to peace and we can sort out and make good decisions. Don't forget how to get to this place, it's a good place to know about for many reasons.

Let's reflect back to the days when the wind could have easily blown your flame out. It is quite a different situation now. There is no way your fire is going out now. The wind will always be there, sometimes positive but more often negative. It is something we all have to deal with but now it's different. You know exactly how to deal with the wind. What to absorb and what to let bounce off of you. Remember what we said about others being where you were yesterday. If you see someone struggling, try to talk them through it. If you are wondering why I keep pointing you towards others, it's because it's a great thing to do. It also helps you more than you think.

Take a look at those questions this morning and see if there are any changes you want to make. Are your answers still the best answers? Are they excellent? Do the same thing for your weaknesses outline. Take some time and really go through them. Look for anything that you don't agree with and make changes as necessary.

Let's take one more look at that flame of yours before we get moving today. Look at how it has grown. Imagine if you could help others build a fire like yours, would you? I ask, because you can help others. The reason I wrote this book is so that I can help others build their fire. If you find yourself with the opportunity to help someone, help them.

The Afternoon

It's the afternoon of day fourteen, hopefully you were able to help a few people or at least observe them and wish them well. You may be surprised how little it takes to help someone. Often a smile or a kind word will make a huge difference in how someone's day turns out.

This afternoon, I want you to take your questions outline and your weakness outline and put them side by side. I want you to look at the first question and your first weakness and determine which is more important. Which one of these two top priority items is more important for you to work on. On a new sheet of paper, we will begin to transform these two outlines into one. We will call it "The Goals". We will start with the same format as before but we will have a few extra levels before we are finished.

This afternoon, we will only work on the top two goals. If the first goal is a weakness then write it out beside the number one. If it's a question then find a way to word it and turn it into a goal. Example: If the question is "What information will I feed my flame?" change it to "Find the best information to fuel my determination because it means everything". This helps us see it as a goal, instead of a question. We will do the same with the answers to your questions, we will turn them into steps and rewrite them in the same manner. Take your time and do this for the top two things on each list. When you finish, you should have two goals on your sheet with major steps below each of them and then small steps below the major steps.

Focus on these top two goals and write them to suit you. Once we get this transformed, we will work hard to accomplish these goals. We will pour everything we have into it, why? Because If we want to have everything that we want, we have to give everything that we have. Remember the world will tell you not to work hard. The world will tell you that you are a sucker for working hard but you will recognize this as wind and won't allow it to affect you.

Once you have finished your top two goals and you are satisfied with what you have on paper, take a moment to review your flame. Did these goals flare it up? Is there any doubt in your head? Is your mind trying to tell you that you can't accomplish these goals? Remember how we deal with the mind when it tries to protect us. Turn your attention directly towards the fear and pull it apart. Dissect it completely. Don't wait, destroy that fear, anxiety and doubt immediately. If we wait, we allow it to grow and fester.

A STORY FROM MY OWN DAY FOURTEEN

On day fourteen I ran with little to no pain. I also had little to no energy and every step I took seemed to completely drain me. I told myself that it would improve when I started to wake up and sweat.

I continued to run but with very little enthusiasm. My mind began trying to talk me out of finishing the run and the challenge. Why are you doing this? What difference will it make? How nice would it be to turn around and go home? I let my mind talk for a minute but I didn't really entertain the idea of quitting.

As I was ignoring the mental traps my mind was setting for me, I started to feel physical pain as well. I kept going but I now turned my focus to the physical pain. I started to break it apart. Where exactly was it coming from? What power does it have over me? Is it real pain or just another mind trap? As I focused on the pain, it began to fade so I thought I would give it a try for the mental side of things.

I focused on my energy level, why is it so low? What is draining my energy? I seemed to feel a little better. I turned my focus to the "let's quit" questions my mind was asking me and I answered them. I'm doing this because I want to, because it will make me a better person and because I can. This will make a huge improvement to my character strength which will improve everyone that I influence. And finally, if I were to turn around and go home, I would only sit there and mentally kick myself in the butt for just sitting there.

It's important to know that I have lost these battles in the past but never during a thirty day self-challenge. I've lost this battle on everyday tasks. I've even lost this battle when the task in question was something fun but I stayed home instead.

In this case, my determination, my flame was too strong to allow me to lose this battle. I won this battle easily but I learned a little something as well. I learned another way to fight this battle.

DAY FIFTEEN

THE MORNING

I t's the morning of day fifteen, the day that marks our halfway point and you should take a few minutes to reflect back over your journey so far. If you are letting go of a habit, think back to when the cravings were so strong that you knew you couldn't win. You were certain that you couldn't resist the urges but you told yourself that you would fight the battle anyway. You did the hardest thing, at the moment when you were sure to lose, you fought. And you are still fighting and that's something to feel great about. If you are forming a new habit, look back to when you weren't committed like you are now. You were just as susceptible to your cravings and urges but they were a little different. Your cravings and urges were trying to keep you in bed or on the couch or whatever you were doing. You weren't serious about your challenge and you didn't really even care if you succeeded. After all, who was going to make you do it? The halfway mark means just as much to you, even though your journey gets difficult as time goes by, you have already committed to this challenge and nothing will stop you from finishing.

No matter which side of this challenge you are on, starting or stopping, I want you to know that you have taken the initial steps toward changing your life. You have resisted the cravings, the wind and overcame your own mind in a battle of "let's just quit". Pretty amazing, but before we congratulate ourselves, let's remember that we are at the halfway point, not finished. The real congrats will be rightfully given at the end of the challenge.

As you get moving this morning, let's take a quick look back at the new outline, "The Goals". Read over it and decide if it still makes sense. Does it still seem to be something that you would want to build from? Don't bother looking over the questions or weaknesses outlines, we have been over those enough already. The important thing right now is to get these goals transformed into a working outline that you can easily refer to later. When I said I wanted to help you change your life, I didn't just mean for thirty days. I want to have a positive effect on you future for a long time.

Now that we have reviewed our first two goals, let's go back to your flame. Take a moment to feel it and see what is happening. What effect did reaching the halfway point have on your determination? Is it burning and growing even more? When you think about your goals, does it flare up? Remember, your goals are the things that will feed this determination and it is directly linked to your passion. I like to see a little flare up when I think about accomplishing my goals.

Again, as you go through your day, look for others that may be facing a difficult moment in life. Take the time to speak to them and talk them through it, if you have the opportunity. Don't get me wrong, you don't need skills for this. Don't offer solutions, just hear them and relate to them. Talk about difficult moments from your own perspective and if they as "what did you do?" then tell them. If it turned out badly, tell them that too. Often, people just want someone to listen and that's enough to help them through a tough time. While you are helping someone, take a peek at that flame. Did it flare up a little? Don't be alarmed, it doesn't mean you are trying to get something from them. That is a sign of leadership. I'm not going to get too deep into leadership right now but I will say that it's the thing that I'm most passionate about. I have studied it, practiced it and improved on it for years now. It is one of the reasons that I write.

The Afternoon

So we have finished off the morning of day fifteen and we have easily defeated any cravings or urges that have attacked us. If our minds tried to weaken us, we just plowed through it and kept going. We can win this battle and still smile at our peers as we walk by. Does that mean the battle is over? Not yet, there will be moments that will test you. You will find weakness in yourself that you didn't know was there and the wind will come and go. Even after you finish your challenge, the wind will still tell you things that are negative. Remember, the wind doesn't want to feel like a lesser person and if you get away with being awesome, there must be a reason. A reason that they aren't doing it. You have some ability that they don't have.

This afternoon, I want you to review your goal outline and get your mind into it. Once you are focused on your goals, I want you to work on the next two goals. We will do this the same way we did yesterday. Look at the second question and second weakness and determine which one is priority. When you make a decision, list that one as goal three and the other as four. Re-word them so that they are a goal instead of just a question or a weakness. Make them into a target that we can shoot for. Then do the same for the major steps and the small steps. Remember to take your time with this and make it excellent.

Once you have finished your goals, I want you to take a break and just think about everything that has happened in the last fifteen days. Are you happy with your progress? Do you think you are a changed person? Do you feel like the challenge is almost over and you aren't sure what to do next? I know I did during my first challenge. I felt great about finishing my challenge but I also felt sad that it was halfway over. It made the ending seem real and I was unsure about what to do next. I didn't want to go back to the old me so I decided not to. I decided to take the new me and run with it. I expect you will do the same and with the plan we will have laid out for you, it will be a great new you.

If you still feel a little sad about the end of the challenge, start thinking about your next challenge. Your next thirty-day challenge, what will it be? What do you want to change? This can be independent from your goals or it can be used to work toward your goals. You can do more than one challenge at a time or you can focus on only one. The challenge is pretty universal. Since my first challenge, I have kept at least one challenge going constantly. There are a thousand small things I want to change about myself and many major things as well. If you look closely at yourself, you will find things you want to improve as well.

We will talk more about the aftermath later. For now, let's take another look at that flame. Feel it and decide what it needs next? We already know you have goals that are fueling it but what else does it need? Think back to what I said about leadership and see what that does for your flame. I don't mean being a boss, I mean really leading. Does it flare up? Enough on that for now, I'm only planting a seed to see if it grows.

31

A STORY FROM MY OWN DAY FIFTEEN

D ay fifteen was very similar to day fourteen, I'm up and running but with little energy and little drive. The commitment to finishing this challenge is the only reason I'm running at all. There is no piece of me that wants to quit, there is only the road and suffering until the timer stops.

I begin to analyze my drive, why is it so low? Two days ago, I was as driven as any other high performer in the world and now I'm having to push myself to finish a simple morning run. Running isn't easy but it doesn't require math, extensive research or any real mental stress, in fact, running usually helps me relieve stress so why am I so unmotivated as I run this morning?

There is no real reason that I can come up with other than maybe I'm a little worn down from fifteen days of this. The thought of doing it for fifteen more days doesn't make it any better. When we feel the same pressure every day, we barely notice it but we may be wearing down a little each day. Eventually, our drive is lowered in order to force us to rest. We talked about being battle weary before, well this is what it feels like.

During this run, I never considered quitting and after the run, I compared my time and distance to other runs. I was pretty consistent with other runs but in my mind I felt like I sucked today. I went a little farther with this dissection and I determined that we are able to make it through these weak moments. The key is to keep moving because if we stop, we may not have the drive to start again. It is also important to pay attention to these moments, if they start happening too often, it may be time for a break. We all need a recharge in some way or another.

32

DAY SIXTEEN

THE MORNING

On the morning of day sixteen, you wake up feeling energized and victorious because you have crossed the halfway line. The days will pass by a little faster now. You finished mile four and went to mile nine of your ten mile race. While you should allow yourself to feel great, you should also remember that we are only half way. I refer you back to the phrase "never congratulate yourself on a job half done". We will congratulate ourselves when the job is finished but for now, we will extract a little happiness from the halfway victory and move on.

As we move into the second half of your challenge, we tend to feel a surge of energy. New found energy is a good thing and we want to use it while we have it. I want to be cautious about using that new energy to try to rush forward. I find that I often try to rush ahead of the situation. I want to get it knocked out so that I can relax and not have a task staring at me while I'm relaxing. The truth is that when we rush ahead, we stand a good chance of missing out on the now. Rushing ahead can also cause some quality issues, if we are talking about rushing ahead on a project.

Now that we talked about what not to do with our new energy, let's discuss what we should do with it. I want you to use that energy to find a way to accomplish the first goal on your list. We still have much work to do on the goals outline but getting started of the details of accomplishing the top priority goal is key. We talked before about the momentum you are building. When you combine new energy with momentum, the results are stunning.

As you go through your day, I want you to keep goal number one in mind. Keep your eyes open for things that could help you accomplish it. Small things, big things and even indirect things are useful at this point. The idea is to make progress towards the goal, nothing else. So don't be afraid to ask others for help. In fact, you should have mentor type people that you can go to with questions. People that you can share your story and goal with and ask for help. If you don't have any mentors, then spend your day today looking for someone that may fit that position. The important thing is to get started working towards goal one.

As you find ideas and possible ways to accomplish your written down goal number one, add a level to your outline under each step. Use a dot and write the detail beside it. Determine which step the detail applies to and list it under that step. If it applies to several steps, then list it under each step that it applies to. Continue this until you have all of the details of the day written down. There will likely be plenty more details so you may want to leave room or consider using a Word document.

The Afternoon

On the afternoon of day sixteen, let's take a quick moment to check our cravings and urges. How did they feel this morning? Did the halfway point make them even weaker? Or did they seem to flare up in an attempt to slow you down? How did you respond to them? Did you feel an urge to quit? Or did you just barrel through them and it seemed like nothing? Again, there are no wrong answers, I want to make sure you have a mental assessment of where you stand against your cravings and urges at this point in the challenge.

So you went through your day with goal one in mind and you began to list some details that will help you accomplish each step. These details are the little things that will lead up to each step and each step will take you closer to accomplishing your goal. This outline will not carry you through your journey but it will serve as a roadmap to help you through unfamiliar territory. There will be times when you will sit back and not know what to do next. During these times, you will look at your outline and see where you stand. Then you will look at your steps and details and pick the best place to get started. I know it sounds simple and it really is but we rarely do the simple things without some encouragement. And when things get complicated, the simple seems to get complicated as well. This will help you navigate through the complicated times with simple precision.

Now I want to go back to your outlines and work on the next two goals. Again, take question number three and weakness number three and assign a priority to them. It will be goal five and six. Convert everything over as we did before and make sure you keep excellence in mind. The last thing we need is a roadmap that doesn't lead us where we want to go.

When you finish with your outline for the night, Take a look at that flame of yours. How is it burning? Is it burning bright enough? While you are assessing your flame, lets weigh it next to a few other things. Determination is everything you ever wanted but determination is made up of a few things. One key component of determination is discipline. Specifically, self-discipline. It's very hard to accomplish anything without self-discipline. I won't say much else about it because you have already demonstrated self-discipline during this challenge. Another key component of determination is persistence. Persistence is doing one thing many times vs doing many things one time. Again, you have shown persistence during this challenge. I want you to keep these things in mind when you look at your flame. There are other components but for now, let's think about discipline and persistence.

33

A STORY FROM MY OWN DAY SIXTEEN

Day sixteen started off with no pain, great energy and a sense of victory for getting through the last couple of low energy days without slacking off. I also felt a sense of accomplishment for making it through the half-way point but I quickly dismiss it. I remind myself not to congratulate myself on a job half done.

Yesterday, I thought about pushing through the low energy times and how to deal with them and today I'm thinking about the reward that comes after pushing through something difficult. One of the greatest feeling I know is the victorious feeling after winning a battle with your own mind. It is an opportunity to see directly into the process of success.

Its early morning, I'm running along with no pain and I'm happy. I am enjoying every step of the run and I can already tell it's going to be a great day. It occurs to me that not everyone will have the great day that I'm about to have. Some will have days like I had the last two days. I decide that I should try to pass along some of my good fortune to the others that may be suffering today. While I can't hand out slices of happiness, I can smile and speak to everyone I encounter. I've had a smile from a happy stranger improve my day in the past, maybe today is the day I can return the favor.

I want to note that I generally try to smile and speak to everyone I encounter every day, even on my bad days. But on a great day, I should be able to really help someone out. As I go about my day, I try to keep noticing that I'm having a great day instead of taking advantage of it. I guess I'm going back to the "in the moment" thing again!

34

DAY SEVENTEEN

THE MORNING

On the morning of day seventeen, I ask you to slow down and take in the day. Don't just see the finish line and do whatever it takes to cross it, really take the time to live today. This falls in line with the "don't rush forward" that we talked about on day sixteen but now I want you to feel every moment of the day and see how it effects your day. I really want to know how it effects the end of your day, but we will have to come back to that this afternoon. For now, just try not to miss anything.

Let's start the morning off with another talk about helping others. As you go through the day, I would like you to see others and try to help them. I know we did this recently and I keep telling you to do this forever, but it really is the best thing that you can do for them which is in turn, the best thing you can do for yourself. While you are out helping others and feeling the day, try to see yourself in others.

Take a look at others and put yourself in their shoes. When you walk into a meeting and see a new co-worker that seems intimidated, try to feel their anxiety and tension. If you were in their shoes, what would you want them to do? How would you want to be treated? What can you do to make them feel more comfortable? When you determine what and how you would want to be treated, approach them and see if you can help. Remember that it takes action to actually help someone. You can think about it all day but unless you actually help them, they are still in the same position.

Now let's take a brief look at your goals outline. Read over all six of your goals and see how they make you feel. Do they make you feel like you are building a roadmap into your future? Do they seem like you are overdoing it a little? If so, don't worry, they seem unnecessary until you are in a rut and need help to figure out which way to go. You don't use Google to find your way home everyday but when you don't know where you are going or you are lost, you are following every step Google gives you. It works the same with this road map, we just must build the map first. Consider yourself the "Google car", building roadmaps for yourself and others.

Before you get started on your day, let's take a look at that flame of yours. Are we building your determination? Are we fueling your fire with the right things? If you look ahead and see your goals and your flame flares up, you are right on target. If we did our job right before, we should have found your passion and formed these goals around that. Remember your goals will change but you should be able to pursue them until you achieve them before letting them go, unless something drastic happens. Then you will have to alter the unfinished goal. When I say something drastic, I mean like losing a leg when your goal was to run a marathon. And by alter the unfinished goal, I mean finishing it in a wheelchair on a prosthetic leg. Whatever it takes to accomplish the goal. Getting as new girlfriend or boyfriend is not a good enough excuse to not accomplish your goals. Anyone you invite into your circle should be willing to help you achieve your goals and then set new ones that will challenge you.

The Afternoon

On the afternoon of day seventeen, take a moment to recap your day. Were you able to move a little slower? Did it influence your day? Maybe you feel more fulfilled because you were "in the moment"? I don't expect you to go slow everyday of your life but occasionally it is a good thing to take a day and enjoy it. I value a sense of urgency more than I can express so this exercise is difficult for me. It is almost torture for me to slow down and take in everything that happen. Often, I look back at the end of the day and it's a blur. I can remember everything that happened, but I really have to stop and think about it. Therefore I put so much energy towards reflection time.

Let's take a quick look back at your day of helping people. Were you able to find anyone that looked uncomfortable and help them? If so, how did they respond? Were you able to help them? How many people were you able to help? When you were helping others, did you see yourself in those people? Did helping others teach you anything? For myself, I always learn something new when I'm teaching or mentoring someone else. No matter how much I study something, when I teach it, a light bulb always lights up and teaches me something I missed. That's not why I like to help others, but it is a happy side effect.

Let's go back to your outlines and repeat the process that we have been using for the last few days. Today, I want you to go ahead and finish up your goals outline. Take your next question and weakness and determine which the priority is. Then list it as we did before. Do this until you get finished with all your questions and weaknesses. If you have more of one then you don't have to worry about comparing the question to the weakness and assigning priority, just list them in order of priority.

When you finish with your goals outline, let's move on to your flame and see how it is looking. By now you are used to seeing a nice size flame with healthy growth. You have been fueling your determination with the right stuff. Keep your flame in mind and think about the times today when you were helping someone. What did it do for your flame? Did if burn a little hotter?

While you are assessing your flame, I want you to again look for other things that your determination is made up of. See the discipline involved and see the persistence we talked about before. Now I want you to see something else inside that flame of determination. This one is as important as any. It's called action. Nothing happens without action. We can be the most motivated and smartest people in the world but if we fail to act, we may as well be fools. As you call it a night and prepare to rest, I would like you to give some thought to action. It's a simple word but it's a key word. During the day on day seventeen, did you take action every time you had the opportunity? If not, what are you going to do about it tomorrow?

35

A STORY FROM MY OWN DAY
SEVENTEEN

It's day seventeen and I'm up and running earlier than usual. I have a ten hour road trip to Midland, Tx. Planned for today. I'm curious how my legs will feel after a run this morning and then riding for that long. I'm feeling great and feeling no pain as I run this morning.

I turn my attention to the trip ahead of me and run through my own personal mental checklist. Do I have everything we need for this trip? Do I have enough cash, just in case we end up in a place that doesn't accept credit cards? Do we have clothes, bathroom amenities, medication and everything else? As I run, I send myself a quick email with the things I may have forgotten. Hind sight update – I did forget to pack warm clothes. I had no idea that the temperature was going to be forty degrees colder in Midland!

After my assessment, I let my mind wander wherever it wants to go. I find myself thinking about the run yesterday and the day before and so on. I start to assess the entire journey that this challenge has taken me on and I find that I'm enjoying it. Even those hard days are enjoyable in hindsight. I dig a little deeper and I find that not only am I enjoying the journey but I'm enjoying the process. Enjoying the process is key to a healthy balance.

Often, we are in such a rush to get the thing finished that we barely even notice the process. We hurry and finish our work, we rush to clean the house and we rush to get through traffic and we really aren't even aware that we are rushing. We are so focused on the end result that we forget to enjoy the process. Take a look at what it takes to build and time an internal combustion engine and then look at all of the traffic around you. It's a whole new perspective on traffic. After we finish rushing, what then? Do we get some reward for getting home ten minutes earlier? Do we get a cleaner house because we rushed or did we sacrifice a little quality?

As you are rushing through your task, remember to pay attention to the process because that's where the magic happens.

36

DAY EIGHTEEN

THE MORNING

On the morning of day eighteen I want you to get started with an open mind. In other words, I'm asking you to be coachable. I know how it sounds but the truth is that we do get to decide. We also get to choose our attitude and I'm asking you to choose a positive attitude this morning. Starting your day off with an eagerness to learn and spread positivity is its own reward. If you benefitted in no other way than that, it would be worth it to start off positive and coachable. It is important to start off everyday in the right mindset but for now, we are talking about today.

We have been out the last few days trying to notice others that are in need or people that could use a little kindness and you have been helping them. Today, I want you to keep looking but I want you to do it with a leadership perspective. Now I realize that if you have never led before that this may seem ridiculous, but the truth is that you must start somewhere. It takes years to become a great leader, but to learn, it only takes getting started. In reality, you have been performing some of the duties of a leader for the past few days. Seeking out others that may need help is something a leader would do. Helping others is something a leader would do.

Now let's get started doing other things a leader would do. Start by following up with the people you helped over the last few days, if you can find them or know them. Find out how they are doing and see if you can help them again. A leader will always follow up and ensure the person in need was doing better. Next let's seek out a mentor, if you already have a leadership mentor (someone you can learn to lead from) then let them know that you are interested in learning to be a great leader. This doesn't mean you have to be a leader, but it is important to know what it feels like and what to do when you look back and see people following you.

When you approach a potential mentor, be sure you are ready to sell them on the idea of mentoring you. What I mean is, don't walk up and say something about them being a mentor and not have anything else to say. Be prepared in detail to tell them what you are doing. Talk about your reasons, your interests and how they will be able to help you specifically. Be prepared to answer the "why me" question. Don't give some line with the intent of flattery, give them an honest answer that comes from the truth. Remember that teaching someone is one of the best ways to learn and it is highly likely that your mentor knows this.

On day Eighteen, remember that we are learning about leadership. The reason you need to know this is that others are following you and you don't even realize it. When you start accomplishing things, people notice, and they follow. If people are going to follow you, you had better be ready to lead, even if it is only leading them to someone else.

Before you hit the road and start learning and leading, take a moment and read over your goals. Does everything look like you want it to? You can rewrite it if you like, in fact, you will almost surely rewrite it often. Especially if you only use it occasionally. Why? Because your growth will always give you a better way. You will also accomplish these goals and need to update as you go. I recommend crossing off your goal with a line that leaves it legible and adding to the bottom of the list. This will leave you a record of where you have been as well as help you in the future.

Now, let's focus for a minute on your flame, how is your determination level? Are you gaining discipline and persistence? Are you taking action on the things that you are determined to do? Keep your flame in mind as you go through your day learning and leading. See how it reacts to different interactions.

The Afternoon

This afternoon on day eighteen, I want you to reflect on your day of learning and leading. Were you able to follow up with anyone from your previous encounters? Did you contact a mentor? During your follow up, how did the person seem? Were they in a stronger position? Did the mentor take you seriously? Were you able to sell the mentor on what you are trying to do? If not, have you dissected the situation and discovered why? How will you try to sell him the next time you see him? These questions are relevant because they will give you the perspective of a leader. In other words, you can put yourself in the leader's shoes for a moment. I realize that many of you are leaders and may have this perspective already. That being said, it will put you back into the right perspective. While we are still on the leadership train of thought, Take a moment and ask yourself if you approached people in the right way. Did you provide solutions to them or did you listen to them? And by listen, I mean really listen, like what they had to say really meant something to you. These leadership exercises are going to help make you a leader or in some cases, make you a better leader At the very least, you will need to know how to lead yourself.

Now let's look back at your outline. Did you do anything productive towards it today? When you were in a spot that you needed direction, did you look at your goals? Probably not, because you aren't used to having this tool. Now that you do have this tool, we may as well make it the best it can be. Try to think back to the moments today where you could have benefitted from some direction. During those moments, what would have helped you? When you figure that out, write it down and then see where it applies to your goals. If it applies to none of them then keep it as a note. If it applies to several of them then list it under each one that it applies to. These are experienced steps and they are very useful during moments of doubt.

Before we finish off the afternoon of day eighteen, let's look back at that flame of determination. How did it react today while you were learning and leading? Is your fire brighter than ever? Are you enjoying your new level of determination? If you don't feel a huge difference, then I urge you to take some time to reflect to the beginning of this challenge. Back to when you were about to cave in to the cravings and urges at any given moment. When you were weaker than you are now. You have become a beast. Your discipline is growing, your persistence has increased, and your determination is on fire. You are taking action by leading, learning and studying. You have studied and written your goals out. You now have a road map of where you want to go. These are huge improvements over where we started! We still have a ways to go but when you look how far we've come, its pretty amazing.

37

A STORY FROM MY OWN DAY EIGHTEEN

D ay eighteen, it's five am in Midland, Texas and I'm up and running. My old friend, pain, has returned. The pain actually showed up about five hours into the road trip yesterday. Not only did the pain show up but it brought a cold front with it. When we drove away from home, the temperature was in the eighties and when we made it to Dallas, it was in the fifties. As we drove further west, the temperature kept dropping.

When I booked this hotel, I saw a picture of a small gym with a treadmill so I assumed that I would be running indoors. After a little stroll throughout the hotel, I found that the picture was a lie so it's off to the street I go. I'm running along with my pain and cold weather and it's not so bad. I should add that I was totally unprepared for cold weather and I'm running in a tee shirt and shorts. This may have been worse but my pain is masked by the unfamiliar environment and the importance of today's activities. Our hotel is next to the airport but it's also kind of remote. I run past building after building and they are all abandoned, industrial type buildings. It's like running through a ghost town.

As I run along, my thoughts focus on the trip we made yesterday. It was a good trip but it was long and tiring. Traffic was not much of a problem until we reached Midland. The weather was a little rainy but not bad for a road trip. All in all, it was a scenic and peaceful trip across Texas. I turn my thoughts to the upcoming meeting ahead. There are a lot of variables involved with getting to this meeting and convincing the parties involved to do business with us.

I end my run by thinking about what I can do to make this trip special for the lovely lady that was willing to endure the long ride with me. I think of a few things and email myself to ensure I don't forget. It's important to note that I was a loner for many years and I appreciate the feeling of accomplishment when you do something all alone but it pales in comparison to the feeling of having someone that you can share everything with.

The lesson I learned on day eighteen was simply balance. We make sacrifices for our careers and we should also make sacrifices for our families and loved ones. If I made a million dollars on this trip and failed to put a smile on my lady's face, did I win? I leave it up to you to decide.

38

DAY NINETEEN

THE MORNING

I t's day nineteen and here you are, approaching the two thirds mark of your journey. Tomorrow marks another milestone that you will feel great about. Today however, you get to feel great just because you want to. Take a moment to feel how those cravings and urges barely even phase you now. While they will try to break you occasionally, they don't stand a chance. It's an easy battle for you now that you have sharpened your skills.

As you go through your day, I want you to pay attention to the priority level of activity that you focus on. If necessary, make written notes. IF you have fifty different tasks in front of you, maybe you should take written notes but if you only have three, mental notes will suffice. These notes don't need to be detailed, they only need to state the time that you started the activity and the time you finish the activity and the level of priority you place on the activity. Let's use the number one for the task with the lowest priority level and a three for the tasks with the highest level of priority. Try to capture everything. If you are saving the world from six am till seven am then note the times and label it as a three. If you are on Facebook or watching videos then note the times and label it as a one. Pretty simple, just make sure you keep track of it throughout the day.

Before you get started with your day, let's go over your goals again briefly. You don't need to spend much time doing this, just read over them so that they are fresh in your mind. Next take an assessment of your flame. This doesn't need to be a time consumer either, just take a moment to think about your determination. Set your discipline level where you want it to be, don't allow it to be set by the day. Own your discipline. Next, check your persistence and finally, determine the level of action you will perform at today.

One other thing I would like you to think about today is attitude. Check your attitude and see how you are starting off. Are you angry at every car you pass on the road? If your tooth paste fell off your tooth brush, did you cuss at it? Do you feel defeated when something doesn't fall into place? If you are feeling this way then you should take a moment to yourself. Use the exercise you once used on your cravings. Find a spot where you won't be disturbed and breathe. Close your eyes and hear the noises around you. Use the noise as a background and then start to think about why you are angry. Is there a reason for you to be angry? If so then dissect it. If not, then decide not to be angry anymore. Ask yourself if you are willing to be angry, defeated or rushed for the entire day? Decide not to allow outside forces to choose your attitude. Choose the attitude you want, right here and now. Now open your eyes and keep this attitude for the entire day.

The Afternoon

So, here we are on the evening of day nineteen and you are still beating this challenge. Not only are you beating the challenge but you are transforming into a better version of yourself. I remember saying that starting is one of the most important parts of your challenge and that is true but it's not the only important step. Not only is starting not the only important step, it's not even the hardest step. The hardest step is continuing day after day until it's over. That's the part where the winners are built and that's where you are right now. Maybe you are already a winner and this is just anther way to win, either way, it's a great thing.

Let's take a look at your day. I want you to make three columns on your notepad with one, two and three on the top of the columns. Now add up the total time for all the priority level ones you spent time on today and write that number under the number one column. Do the same thing for priority level two under column two and priority level three under column three. When you finish, take an honest look at how much time you spent doing priority level one activity. Is it much more that priority level two and three? It should be. If it isn't then you will need to restructure your time management.

There are many ways to structure your time management. One way is through delegation. Delegation is hard for many people because it involves passing a task to someone else. As human beings, we want to carry our share of the load and it's counterintuitive to pass tasks to others. This is not a quality that you will have the luxury of keeping in the future. Delegating something doesn't mean passing the buck at all. It means utilizing the entire team and helping others to grow. How can you expect others to grow and get to where you are if you never give them a chance to do the thing? Being a passenger will let you see all of the steps involved but it will never let you get the feel of driving. Learn to delegate. If done correctly, it will be helpful to you and appreciated by the person you are trusting. You must be ready to support the person that you are delegating to and be prepared to coach them.

Another way to structure your time management is to prioritize. You should be pretty good at this by now. As much as you possibly can, work on your priority level one activities first. In other words, get the important things finished and if something gets left undone, make sure it is a level three priority. This ensures that the critical parts of your day are completed on time. There are many books and other materials out there that can help with time management, if you decide to take it to the next level.

Now let's turn our focus to your attitude of the day. How did choosing your own attitude work out? If it worked out then great but if it didn't then don't despair. It takes some practice to set your own attitude and keep it all day. We will be practicing as we go and I know you will get better at it.

Lastly, let's look at your flame. Is it burning at the level of determination you think it should be? Are the activities and exercises we have been doing fueling it the way you want them to? Are there any changes you would like to make that would help you become more determined? If so, then by all means make the changes. You can and will always change. Change is a part of life and resisting it only gets you left in the past.

39

A STORY FROM MY OWN DAY NINETEEN

D ay nineteen and I'm up and running in Midland Texas again. It is not as cold as it was yesterday, and the pain seems to have eased up a little. A simple thing like the wind in my face makes me happy this morning. I have a slight hangover, but I easily dismiss it and forget about it. Not today hangover, come back when my challenge has been completed!

As I run today, it occurs to me that there are many people that would love to run this morning but for some reason, they are unable to do so. It could be a disability or an injury or maybe that they cannot win the battle with their own laziness. Whatever the reason is, I'm sure it's a serious reason, if it prevents them from doing what they want. I feel bad for those that will never experience the feeling that I feel this morning as I run.

On day nineteen, I remembered to be thankful for the abilities and opportunities I have.

40

DAY TWENTY

THE MORNING

I t's day twenty of your thirty-day challenge and you are standing
on the two thirds mark. What an amazing accomplishment! You
should take a moment to let that sink in. Enjoy the moment and
feel great about what you have done. Another milestone passed and
another day closer to the win. How does it feel? Is it a little bitter
sweet because you may not want it to be over? Or are you ready for
the pressure to be off you? Either way, remember that when this challenge is over, you are far from finished. If you just ended a nasty habit,
the last thing you want to do is start doing it again. And, if you just
started a great habit, you will want to continue it forever. Maybe not
with the same intensity but you don't want to let go of a good habit.

As you get started on day twenty, remember back to what we
learned about momentum. You are two thirds of the way finished and
you should have a ton of momentum behind you. It would be hard to
stop now even if you wanted to. You are a locomotive moving forward
at full speed. Unstoppable comes to mind when I think about where
you are in this challenge. No matter what happens, you will find a way
to finish this challenge and finish it strongly.

Moving on to a thought for today. Let's use responsibility for
today's focus. Responsibility is defined as the state or fact of being

accountable or to blame for something. Today, let's practice responsibility. Assume you will have to give a detailed answer for everything you do today. Take a moment to feel that for a moment, in your mind. If you make today great, you will be able to give an answer that makes the world a better place. If you screw up, then you will have to answer for that as well. Which path will you take? If you answered, I don't know yet then you missed my point on day nineteen. We aren't going to let the world decide if we are going to give a great report or a terrible one. We are going to decide right now.

We are also going to decide to have a great attitude again. Our attitude will flow from the inside out, not the other way around. When we decide to own our attitude, we are accepting responsibility for it, so we are getting off to a great start with accepting responsibility as well. The point in this is to learn to choose our attitude every day and to treat every situation as if we are responsible for it. This will help us to take action, every time an opportunity arises which will improve pretty much our entire lives.

And the last thing before you begin day twenty. Take a close look at those goals and see if they are still solid. If they aren't, you can still change them but only if they don't fit anymore. Never change a goal because you didn't want to work hard for it. Often, after we start applying discipline, responsibility and leadership to our daily lives, we transform a little and some goal adjustment may be necessary. It is always ok to change, if you are changing for the right reasons. Never let weakness be a reason and never let weakness win. If you are too weak to win, get stronger and try again.

The Afternoon

It's the afternoon of day twenty and you have successfully completed two thirds of this journey. It's important to take a moment and see how great it feels to pass this marker. Again, don't congratulate yourself on a job that isn't finished but take some time to reflect and look at how far you have come. It's also important to keep the momentum going and to keep fueling your flame with the right practices, exercises and information.

This morning we talked about being responsibility and attitude and how we would choose our own attitude. We would not let the outside world choose our attitude for us. I would like to add a little something to that this evening. I want you to own your expectations. Sounds simple right? That's because it is simple. So, why do we allow our expectations to float and be determined by the wind and the outside world? Often, we don't even think about expectations until afterwards. Sometimes we are disappointed with the results of an event and we didn't even have any expectations. Today, I want to you to set your own expectations and see how the results measure up. At this point in your challenge, if you have a craving, you fully expect to beat it, right?

Another thing about expectations is that we don't set expectations for others, ever. We just do the thing and whatever happens, happens. When someone is disappointed with the results, we are totally surprised by it. How can we avoid the disappointment and the surprise? One way we an do this it to own the expectations of your actions. Tell people upfront what they can expect. If we do this, expect these results. No one is surprised, and no one is disappointed. You can do this even if you have no idea what the results will be. It goes like this, if we do this, I have no idea what the results will be. Again, no one is disappointed, but you may both be surprised. Even if you are surprised, you will be expecting the surprise.

Let's go back to your goals for a minute. Read over them and think about your day. Did your day's activities align with these goals? Did the things you learned today bring you any closer to these goals. Now that we are practicing discipline, persistence, and owning our attitude and putting in the effort, we should be aware of our activities. The activities of our day should be moving us closer to achieving our goals. This takes some time and patience but it will happen. Keep looking at your goals and reading them every morning and evening and you will begin to alter your routines to fit your goals. If you see something that is counter productive to your goals, do something to change it. Don't allow your daily routine to hinder your goals because the effects can surprising. A bad daily routine can set you back considerably and cause your goals to get further away. When this happens, it's difficult to keep driving towards your goals.

Let's take a look at that flame for a minute. What effect did owning your attitude and responsibility have on it today? Did you see any growth of your determination? Remember that passion is directly linked to your determination. If your flame is flaring, then it's likely that you are following your passion. Make sure you are putting in enough effort and action into your daily activities. There will be days when you will have the urge to be lazy but don't allow it. You are already skilled at dealing with urges, use these skills to keep going during these times.

As we close out day twenty, keep in mind that everything revolves around action and effort. Without these, nothing gets done. I know positive people that are in poor shape because they don't do enough. They would rather be lazy and give in to the urges than fight and be active. If that is what you want then fine but it's unlikely that you would have made it this far, if that were the case. Remember, the sound of everything travels, even the sound of doing nothing.

41

A STORY FROM MY OWN DAY TWENTY

Day twenty and I'm up and running early but instead of the street, I'm on a treadmill. We are staying with family in San Antonio Texas and the apartment complex has a gym. San Antonio is the half way point between Midland and home, so we only drove about six hours yesterday. We are able to visit family and break up the return trip.

We had a nice dinner and drinks yesterday evening mixed with some great conversation and family. I'm sweating out some of that dinner and drinks on the treadmill and I think back to some of the laughs we shared last night and it makes me smile. It's a good thing I'm the only one in the gym because smiling on the treadmill is just creepy!

I'm running with no pain this morning and the treadmill seems to reduce the impact, which makes it even nicer. Even though I'm not on the street where I can see the world as I run, I'm still enjoying it. I focus on my breathing for a few minutes and analyze every inhalation and exhalation. After a few minutes, I open my mind and let my thoughts flow. As each thought occurs, I think about it, file it in the finished pile. I do this over and over and before I know it, my timer is going off. I stop my timer and just keep running because I'm enjoying it. In spite of the challenge and the pressure and wind that it brings with it, I'm enjoying my run.

On day twenty, I learned that I can enjoy what I'm doing, even when I have to do it.

42

DAY TWENTY-ONE

THE MORNING

H ere we are on the morning of day twenty-one, from this point forward, you are counting down single digits. The challenge is winding down quickly but you are still ramping up. I'd like you to take a moment and think about that. What will you do with yourself when this is over? You will have your road map, a lot of knowledge and new skills but what will you do with them? We will discuss this more and more as the challenge moves forward but I want to go ahead and plant the seed now.

Now, let's take a moment to set our attitude, own our responsibility and determine what our expectations are for today. How will your attitude be today? Will you roll with the punches and be bigger than what happens to you? Of course you will, no one wants to be angry, many of us don't set our attitudes and therefore our attitude is set by the wind. Our day is also better when we decide to be responsible for the day. If we are sure that we will have to answer for our actions, our actions are much more positive. And finally, if we set expectations for ourselves, we aren't disappointed or surprised by our results. This woks for others as well. Set the expectation beforehand and avoid the disappointment for them as well.

Now, let's look at our goals. What will we do today that will move us closer to achieving our goals? Remember you have a complete roadmap that will help you decide what the best path forward is. A roadmap that you are updating every time something changes, now that's a roadmap that is helpful! Go over everything and decide if changes need to be made and when you finish, start your day with these goals in mind.

As you go through your day, following your road map, think about what you receive from others. When you interact with someone, notice if they gave you a good feeling. Also notice if you learned something from them. Anything notable about the interaction, make a mental note of it. You may want to think back about it later when you are reflecting. When the interaction is finished, tell the person what you gained from them. Give them credit for it. Always give credit where it is due, unless it's you/ If you deserve the credit, don't accept it from yourself. Only others should give you credit. It's ok to feel good about what you have done and let it warm your heart but taking credit out loud rarely gives us any satisfaction.

Before you get started, take a moment to go over your flame. Think about your goals and let that flame burn. Think about what you will feel this afternoon when I ask you to assess your flame. What could you do this morning that you will be happy to look at this evening? What ever that is, do it.

The Afternoon

On the afternoon of day twenty-one, lets look back over your day. Did your attitude stay where you chose to set it? Or did you allow the wind and the day to change it? If it stayed where you set it then great but if it didn't, keep trying. Remember, it takes practice to become great at setting your attitude. The important thing at this point in your change is that you consciously make an effort to set it.

Now let's turn our attention to your responsibility. Did you own everything you did or influenced today? Explain your day to yourself or think back over it carefully and decide if you were able to give a positive report that would make the world a better place. Or if you must deliver a report about how you could have done better. Either way, study it and determine what you could have done better. Taking full responsibility for all your daily activities and influence is not an easy task, so don't beat yourself up over it. It is a great practice and it will make you a better person. It has made me a better person.

Moving on to discipline now, think about self-discipline for a minute. Self-discipline is defined as the ability to control one's feelings and overcome one's weaknesses. Your self-discipline has gotten you this far along in this challenge because you set your level of discipline at the start of this challenge. You likely did it without even thinking about it. You knew the challenge would be tough, you determined what it would take, and you overcame your weaknesses and controlled your feelings. It's that simple. It is far from easy but it's simple.

Lastly, let's determine what our expectations were for today. If we set our attitude, our determination and our responsibility in the right levels and our self-discipline was high enough, then we should have had high expectations for the day. We should have been satisfied with our results. No surprises, no excuses and no disappointment. That's what you should expect when you set your mind in the right place each day and that is what you will get.

Before we call it a day, let's focus on our goals for a moment, did we get closer? I know we intended to close the gap. How did it work out? Did you find opportunities to use your roadmap? Was it accurate and helpful? This is a good time to make a few changes and tweaks if necessary. When you finish, remember that if you didn't get exciting results today, keep trying. The secret to life is to keep trying. Don't try something twice and then give up on it, try it a thousand times. End your day on this idea – You will become great at whatever you do repeatedly. What do you want to be great at?

43

A STORY FROM MY OWN DAY
TWENTY-ONE

I t's a Sunday and I started a little later than normal so I'm running in the daylight. Yesterday was a long day of driving, unpacking and catching up on everything that stood still while we were away. For me, the driving is the most tiresome part.

I'm not feeling much pain as I run this morning, my body must be adapting to this early morning ritual. I'm a little surprised that I'm in no pain, considering all of the driving and flying I did last week. I'm not complaining about it though! I feel good enough this morning to pick up the pace and see how far I can go before my timer goes off.

As I run, I reflect over the previous week and decide that we made some great strides towards our goals. I can feel a momentum building and I want to make sure we keep it going. Momentum is a great thing, especially when it's behind you and pushing in the right direction.

During times when our energy is low, momentum can help carry us through. Imagine experiencing a five-day low energy period. Without momentum, we may have to play catch-up for weeks to get back to where we left off but with momentum behind us, we can float right on through. Or at least part of the way. Even if you don't float all the way, you will still have much less catching up to do.

On day twenty-one, I felt momentum building and I made a decision to keep it going.

44

DAY TWENTY-TWO

THE MORNING

O n the morning of day twenty-two, I would like to start the morning off with determination. Let's look at your flame and see how it looks right off the bat. Before you even get started on your day, look at your level of determination and decide if it is where it needs to be. Could you be more determined? If so, then how do we get there? What can you do to increase your level of determination? One thing you can do is decide. Decide your level of determination now rather than let it be decided for you during the day. If you need a starting point, then say this "I'm going to be determined enough today to accomplish my every day duties as well as two steps that will bring me closer to my goal. That should be challenging but reasonable. Maybe even add a little more clarity by choosing which two steps they will be.

When you have chosen the steps you will take this morning, don't allow anything to stop you from achieving them.

Now that you know what you will do, and you are determined to do it. Will you do it with a smile or with a frown? How do you want this day to go? Will you be focused on the pain of having extra things to do or will you see it as an opportunity to be able to do them? Will you set your attitude now or will you allow others and circumstances to set it for you? Let's just go ahead and set it now. Decide to be happy, coachable and helpful. Decide that you will accept every challenge that presents itself to you with a smile and a positive attitude.

Now, let's decide to own the day. Let's make today ours and be responsible for it. If I have a bad day and have to report out on it, I will have to say that I caused the bad day. Or at the very least, I allowed the day to be bad. Decide this and then do not allow the day to be bad. The day is ours. We own it and even if the wind tries to destroy it, we will make the best of it.

And finally, what do we expect from today? What do others expect? We expect to have a challenging day that will test our abilities and on top of that, we expect to achieve two steps towards our goals. Others will expect us to be great, positive and responsible. Which is exactly what we are because we decided to be. Now let's decide to get started living up to our own expectations and exceeding other's expectations.

The Afternoon

Day twenty-two and you are still knocking it out of the park. You are squashing any cravings or urges that may try to sneak up on you and you are quickly learning how to deal with things that you rarely paid attention to in the past. Things you allowed to form on their own in the past, you are now controlling and changing. You are well on your way to a better you and there is no stopping you.

How did you fare with determination today? Did you stay determined all day or were there times when you seemed to slack off? Perhaps at the end of the day, you were weary, and your determination faded? I say again that your determination is like a muscle that will get stronger and stronger as you continue to use it. Your attitude and responsibility will also get stronger and stronger as you continue. Your persistence will continue to grow, and your expectations will become more accurate as you keep working on them.

Most of us have exercised our body before, either at home or at a gym. When you go to the gym, you work out several muscles, not just one muscle. And you don't just do it once and expect to see results. It takes a little while to see the results and it will be the same here. The question is, when you see the results, how stunning do you want them to be? Do you want mild results, or do you want major results? I already know the answer to that question.

The way to get those major results is to give everything you have. Don't tell yourself that you will give it a shot, that's what people say when they know they will not give it a shot. Tell yourself you will do it. It's that simple. If you give everything you have, you can have everything you want. Keep that in mind this afternoon and ask yourself if you are giving everything you have. Ask yourself if you have ever given everything you have and give it an honest answer.

Before we get too far ahead, stop and think about those two steps from your goals. How did it feel to make some progress? Did it make your determination spike? I didn't ask if you completed these two steps because I already know you did. And if by some chance you didn't finish them, the day isn't over so I have confidence that you will make it happen.

I want to end the afternoon by saying this, you will become great at whatever you do the most. The question is, what do you want to be great at? Is it watching television? Is it complaining about things that don't go your way? I can't think of anyone that really wants to be great at those things or any other things that are like them. Many of us are great at these types of things because that is what we do the most. It's a sad story but it's true. To avoid getting caught up in the traps like this, we need to have healthy hobbies. We will talk more about healthy hobbies tomorrow but for tonight, think about what you do for fun and how much time you spend doing it. If you love what you do for a living, then don't be alarmed if many of these fun things are part of your job. We will go over these thoughts in the morning.

45

A STORY FROM MY OWN DAY
TWENTY-TWO

D ay twenty-two and I'm up and running early and with no serious pain, again. I'm beginning to get used to running without pain. I'm not sure if my body has adjusted to a morning run or if I'm just pumped up because the end of the challenge is near. Either way, I'm enjoying the days of painless running.

It's a Monday morning after a long week of traveling and I'm enjoying a run before work. As I run, I prepare myself for the week ahead. I have many follow ups to complete and I want to finish them ASAP. It's always a challenge to get your head back in the game after a weekend. I find the best way to do it is to just dive right in. Don't test the water, just dive in completely and tackle the toughest task of the day. I go back to a phrase from Mark Twain "Eat a live frog first thing in the morning and nothing worse will happen to you the rest of the day". The point is to do the hard things first, then the day just keeps getting easier.

Next, I allow my mind to focus on the run and the world around me. The view during an early morning run is rarely matched during other times of the day. Even when its dark out, there is still the silhouette of the moon, the stars and the lights of the town.

I turn my thoughts back to this challenge and the changes that have taken place since I started it. I began with a light thought about running for thirty days consecutively with little to no commitment. Later in the challenge, I felt the desire to commit and shortly after that, I did commit. Since I committed to this challenge, I've had several great excuses to stop or to skip a day or even just to take a break in the middle of a run but nothing has even come close to breaking me. I've learned to enjoy running again, manage pain better and I've developed my character by correcting a few fundamental flaws. How great is that?

On day twenty-two, I took the time to measure how far I've come. I was careful not to congratulate myself because the goal isn't accomplished yet but I was happy with the progress that has been made so far.

46

DAY TWENTY-THREE

THE MORNING

G ood morning on day twenty-three. On day twenty-three, I want to start off by enjoying the journey. We have come so far but have we stopped and smelled the flowers along the way? Now is a good time to think about all the good things we have felt, done or been part of on this journey. We have spent much time focusing on the bad stuff like beating the cravings and urges, now that we are in greener pastures, let's focus on the good. Start with the good things that happen to you directly. Think about the good things that have made you happy along your journey. Take a moment to feel those moments and think about your flame. See what those things do to your flame. Now let's turn our attention to the good things that have happened to others during your challenge. What might some of those things be? How did they affect others? How does thinking about this affect your flame?

Now let's talk more about healthy hobbies, I said yesterday afternoon that we would discuss this further and here we are. Let's get started by thinking about an unhealthy habit. Television can be an unhealthy habit if we overindulge. If you add chips and sweets into the mix then it can be even worse. And it can be even worse yet, if we are doing it while we should be doing other things. I'm not anti-television but it is a good example of an unhealthy habit, if its used wrong.

Biking could be an example of a healthy habit. Riding a bike for thirty minutes or an hour every chance you get would be great for you, assuming your current health would allow it. Riding a bike is healthy, good for the heart and is a low impact form of exercise. This is good news for those of us that have previous knee injuries. Other examples of healthy habits can be fishing, running, singing or anything that doesn't degrade your health and keeps you busy and happy. These healthy habits may not be a passion of yours, but they will keep you from becoming great at watching tv. You should already be following your passion during your productive time. These habits are meant to help you fill the gaps with productive time.

As you go through your day today, I want you to pay attention to the things that make you happy. It may be a joke, a story or the way the sun rise catches your eye at a certain time of the morning. Whatever it is, I want you to remember two things while you are enjoying the moment.

First, I want you to know that not everything is meant for everyone. What I mean is, some moments are meant only for the person that is experiencing them. We tend to pull out our phones every time we see something beautiful and try to capture them in a photo. The photo never captures the moment in the same way that it struck you so everyone else that sees it isn't affected in the same way. A beautiful photo of a sunrise through a clearing is much different that turning a corner and having the same beautiful sunrise jump out at you in the clearing. It just isn't the same. So decide if you want to share that moment with the world in a discounted photo or if you want to express it with your words. It is also acceptable to keep some moments all to yourself.

The second thing that I found out about these moments is they are less potent every time you experience them. Meaning that the same sunrise will have less of an effect on you, each time you see it. I'm not telling you this to be negative about these events when they happen. I'm telling you this because I want you to take the time to enjoy these moments the first time they occur. If you had known that that sunrise would be less amazing in the future, you may have enjoyed it for a little longer the first time you saw it. So, take the time to enjoy the moment. If you are riding a bike and you see a beautiful tree in a field that touches you, slow down and enjoy it. Don't assume that you will feel the same way about it tomorrow.

Now, take a moment to set your attitude, own the day and decide what to expect. Remember to help others to do the same thing, if you get the opportunity. Also remember to extract the happiness out of your day and take the time to enjoy it. Something as simple as a happy moment with your son or daughter can make your whole day, if you take time to enjoy it. The world will still be there tapping its foot when you get ready so don't let it rush you!

The Afternoon

On the afternoon of day twenty-three, I would like to go over your day and see what where we can find room for improvement. First, let's take a moment to reflect over your entire day. Find a quiet spot and close your eyes. Turn the background noise into something you can use and just think back for a minute. Don't get caught up or focus in on anything, just see the events of the day from a distance.

Mow that your mind is on the day, let's go over some of the things we were working on yesterday. First off, did you smell the flowers today? When good things happened, did you take a moment to enjoy them? Did you notice all the good things that happen in a regular day of your life? Take a moment to pick a few of those good things and study them. What can you do to make more of those good moments? What about the moments when good things happened to others? Can we make more of those?

Now let's talk about the healthy hobbies. Didi you think of anything you may be interested in? Anything you would like to do other than watch television or play on the phone? If not, just keep it in your mind until you do. Write it where you will see it, send yourself a calendar invite or something that will keep you thinking about it. If you did think of a few ideas then let's add them to your goals. At the bottom, make a new goal called "develop healthy hobbies" then break it down the same as the other goals. List your potential hobbies and the steps it will take to develop them. Work on these during your leisure time.

During your day yesterday, did you find things that make you happy? Remember, it could be anything that just makes you want to smile. When you found something that made you happy, did you enjoy it? I mean, did you stop and enjoy it, or did you take a picture in an attempt to capture the moment? I know this may be counterintuitive to some of us. We want to capture the moment, so we can share it with others and because we want to enjoy it again later. In reality, as I said yesterday, the moment is discounted as soon as we snap the picture. Why? Because as soon as we snap the picture, the moment is no longer a moment. It becomes forever and if you have something forever, there is less reason to feel that it may be a once in a lifetime occurrence.

As we close out the afternoon, I want you to again read over your goals and look for any changes or things that you no longer agree with. Also, consider which steps you will work on tomorrow. Look at your progress so far, how are you doing? When you find yourself unsure about what you should do next, do you think about or read this road map? Remember that we built this to be a resource to you. When we are unsure about what to do, often we will take the easy thing and end up watching tv instead of working towards our goals. This map will always let you know what you should be doing, if you take the time to read over it.

47

A STORY FROM MY OWN DAY TWENTY-THREE

Day twenty-three and I'm on the street running early and again, I'm feeling very little pain. I'm excited to be running with high energy and low pain. This is becoming a habit. Having been a runner for quite some time now, I'm certain that the pain will return soon enough. I decide to just enjoy it while it lasts.

I process the thoughts that I need to keep my schedule on target and my focus on the right things and of course, I send myself an email so that I remember what I need to remember. I then reflect on the events of last week and try to ensure that I didn't miss anything. I'm reminded of a phrase I read in a book by Nick Saban called How Good do you Want to Be. The phrase read "win or lose, let it go and move on within twenty-four hours. I think this is good advice, holding on to a loss hurts our confidence and holding on to a win will prevent us from trying hard enough. The key is to push as hard as you can for the next win, don't hold onto the past. A win today will not get me a win tomorrow and if I lost today, it means that I lost today. It doesn't mean that I suck, it just means I need to try something else.

48

DAY TWENTY-FOUR

THE MORNING

On the morning of day twenty-four, let's start off with attitude, responsibility, expectations and action. Decide what your attitude will be right now. Don't allow the morning to decide. Next decide to own your day and everything you do. And finally, you will take action on every opportunity that comes along. You will spread your great attitude, teach others how to be responsible by setting an example and you will perform the necessary action every time. You will know what to expect from yourself and you will let others know what you expect from them.

Next let's read over your goals and determine what we will choose to complete today. What progress will we make? I won't ask you to complete two steps, I will only ask that you make progress. I don't want to put a lid on you. If you want to complete ten steps today, then do it. If you think one step is your limit for the day, then do that. Make sure you challenge yourself and strive to exceed your own expectations. The expectations you have already set earlier this morning. Also remember that your goals are a live document. Meaning that you will be changing and adding constantly. If you see that a new step needs to be added, add it. If you see that a step or goal needs to be changed then make the change.

As you move along today, try to seek out people that may need your help. Maybe it is the same people from the previous times you set out to help. I bet you can help them even more at this point because you have learned so much and came so far. If these people are coming back to you, then try to help them again. If they aren't coming back to you, then follow up with them and see how they are doing. This is about them and how you can add value to them. Don't try to give answers that you don't know the answer to. Just hear them, relate to what they are saying. If the problem can be solved, try finding an answer and helping them to find an answer but don't just offer up solutions. Helping them find answers is better than trying to cram an answer down their throat.

Last thing for the morning of day twenty-four, let's talk briefly about relaxation. I don't mean laying on the beach and sipping a margarita, as nice as that may sound. I want you to be able to relax as you deal with others. I also want you to relax as you work towards your goals and perform your daily duties. As highly driven people, we naturally tend to rush ourselves and we have a strong sense of urgency. Today, let's learn to relax. There is no rush, unless it's an emergency, and even then, we must relax enough to control the situation. When it isn't an emergency, we will accomplish more and keep going longer, if we learn to relax. So, when you are working on something today and three other things pop up, relax. When it feels like everything is piling up, relax and make smart decisions. Remember, can it be delegated? And focus on the top priorities first. If you don't finish something, you want it to be low priority.

The Afternoon

Now that we made it through the morning, let's review. You started off by setting your attitude, deciding to own the day, setting clear expectations and deciding that you would take action. Were you able to keep everything at the level you set it? IF so, then it was a great day but if not, it was a practice day. It will take some time to master the art of setting your levels and keeping them there. The important thing is that you are setting the levels, paying attention to them throughout the day and correcting yourself as you go. I sometimes catch my attitude slipping and I immediately correct myself. I do this for all my levels, even they have been slipping for several hours, I correct them as soon as I notice the slip.

Let's review your roadmap for a few minutes. Were you able to complete your progress that you marked today? Did you live up to your expectations? If you completed the progress that you expected, was it too easy? Or was it very hard? Try to keep a balance here. If it's too easy, you aren't challenging yourself. This leaves small pieces of energy unused or wasted on low priority level tasks and they add up over time. If it was extremely hard to achieve the expectations, ask yourself if you enjoyed the challenge. If the answer is yes, then continue to set the bar too high. If you had to force yourself to meet those expectations and you find yourself wanting to hurry up and end it then lower the bar and work up from there. Remember, there is no rush, we are looking for progress over time. There may be days when your energy is so high that you knock out many steps and that's great. That is why this is a living document and it's designed to fit you.

While you were helping people and following up, how did that make you feel? Did you set expectations with them? Were you able to help? Did you listen well enough? Do you think they felt like you were the best listener in the world? If not, then why not? If yes, how did you do it? Were you able to help them search for answers? Did they find the answers they were searching for? With your help, I'm sure they found answers.

Let's move on to relaxation. How did you feel this morning when you tried to relax? Was it awkward? Did relaxing help you make smart decisions? Did you find it hard to relax? Were you able to relax every time something new came up? If not, then don't worry, it takes time to learn to relax. I realize that I say this often but it's the truth. It will take some time to do anything worthwhile. The good thing is that we can enjoy the journey. This roadmap is not meant to be a race, think of it as a relaxing drive along the beach. People are everywhere, some are waving as you pass. Sometimes you will find others that could use a helping hand and other times you will be the one that needs help.

What ever the case, learn to relax. Respond to things instead of knee jerk reactions.

Let's evaluate your flame of determination as we end the day. How does it look at this point of your challenge? How did the idea of relaxation affect it? Does knowing that you will be able to relax and enjoy the journey make it burn hotter? How did the follow up and helping others search for answers affect it? End your afternoon thinking about how you can help others relax and make smart decisions.

49

A STORY FROM MY OWN DAY
TWENTY-FOUR

D ay twenty-four and I'm on the street early again. I have a little pain but it's almost like I'm insulated from it. I focus on the pain for a minute and it subsides. I have been running the same path for many years now but this morning I got a little surprise.

Two of my neighbors dogs had escaped from their yard and before I knew it, I was staring at an angry German Shepard and a blue healer. My headphones allowed them to run right up on me without me hearing them. I yelled loudly for them to go home and the German Shepard immediately backed down. He was no longer aggressive, but the healer was a different story. The healer was smaller than the German Shepard, but he was way more aggressive. He came at me snarling and I held my ground. When I took a few slow steps towards him, he lost his nerve and I kept walking at him. He finally backed down but he came at me from behind as I went past. I turned around and kept eye contact with him until he was far enough away to know I wasn't a threat.

I had never met these dogs and they weren't used to being outside of their yard, so it was a bad situation. If I had reacted and ran, I'm certain that I would have been bitten, since I was able to relax and respond, I was able to keep the situation in check. The only reason that the healer didn't attack is because he was sure he would lose. If I hadn't held eye contact and made an aggressive move towards him, his confidence would have flared, and I would have had to get shots and possibly stitches. Also, I would have had to kill my neighbor's dog and that's never a positive thing.

The lesson I took away from this isn't about standing your ground. It's more about choosing the correct response to a situation. In this case, I saved myself a lot of trouble by standing up to the dogs, other situations may have called for a different approach. If the German Shepard had been as aggressive as the healer, I would have had to think of something else. The point is to overcome the fight or flight instinct and respond according to the situation. On day twenty-four, I chose the right reaction.

50

DAY TWENTY-FIVE

THE MORNING

O
n the morning of day twenty-five, we are at the point in your challenge where we only have five days left to go. You are five days from finishing your challenge and you are stronger than ever. Take some time to think back to the earlier days of this challenge and remember how it felt. Now, work your way through the entire challenge up to where you are now and see the differences and the growth pattern. What made you grow faster or slower? What parts of the challenge are you happy about and what parts could you have done better?

Now, let's move on to the start of the day. Set your attitude and don't allow the day to start off the wrong way. What will you do today to make the world a positive place? Next let's decide again to own the day and everything that happens. Next, set your expectation level. What do you expect today? What do you expect from others? Decide that you are going to relax and make smart choices in stead of being tense and in a hurry. You will practice relaxing and make calm, thought out decisions. Remember, there is little value in knee jerk reactions.

Now let's read over those goals and decide if there is anything that is out of alignment. If all is well, you are ready to decide what progress you will make today. What will you do to work towards your goals today? When you decide what you will accomplish, determine how you will do it. When you do it, what do you expect the outcome to be? What affect will it have on others? If there is an effect on others, are they expecting it?

As you go about your day, try to see friends and family as much as possible. If you can't see anyone, call them and catch up with them. Even if they were the wind at the beginning of this challenge, have a conversation with them and let them know that your challenge is nearing its end, and you are still going. Why would I ask you to do this? Because you will have to deal with them at some point and doing it while you are strong in your challenge is a good time to do it. I remember when I quit smoking, I hadn't smoked in months but when I would run into an old friend or family member, I would immediately reach for my cigarettes. Then I would remember that I didn't smoke anymore but I would still have a small craving for a cigarette. In an effort to prevent this or minimize it, you should go ahead and speak to as many people as possible. Some of the people that I would run into had negative stories to tell me. About how they stopped smoking for six months and started back. Or how their cravings and urges never went away and mine wouldn't either. It's best that you face this now rather than later. The truth is, I haven't had an urge to smoke in years. I had mild urges to smoke for a while, but they were easily defeated. I smoked for eighteen years and when I quit, I was up to two and a half packs per day. It wasn't easy, but it was achievable, and I did it. You can do your thing too, but the wind will tell you different!

I will ask you to again, help others when possible. If you know them well enough, ask about their goals. If they don't know, then encourage them to pursue the next level. If they aren't interested, don't push them. If they are interested, then help them get started. I find that most people with any sort of inner drive are very interested in my thirty-day challenge stories. That's because the concept is in alignment with out thought process. A person that has little drive may need to learn or discover drive before they will understand. Some may never understand, and others may be born with drive. Either way, you can improve your drive. One way to increase it is to build a clear roadmap to your future by setting goals and knowing how to accomplish them. Don't try to teach everything at once. Just plant a small seed and if they are interested and ready, they will pursue.

The Afternoon

On the afternoon of day twenty-five, let's review your day in the same order that we set up for it. Before we do, I want to take a moment to feel any cravings you may have had today. If you experienced any urges to do or no do the things, just close your eyes and think about how great it feels to know that you own those cravings and urges. Try to think back to harder times and remember how that felt. Remember that these cravings and urges will completely disappear, but it will take some time. In the meantime, the cravings will be very weak and will continue to fade. I say this so that you aren't surprised, and you know what to expect.

Now, let's address your attitude from the day. Were you able to keep it where you set it? If you had to adjust, did you adjust accordingly? Did you think the adjustment through or did you perform a knee jerk reaction? Think for a moment about all the things you could have improved on. Now let's move on to responsibility, did you own the day? Did you change the things you could control? Did you waste any time trying to change others or did you own the situation and move forward? How about your expectations, were they accurate? How did it go when you were trying to relax? Were you able to stay calm and relax? When you tried it, did it feel right? Or would you feel better in a rush? If you struggled with any of these mindsets, don't be concerned. It takes a while to master these things but when you do, you will control your mind instead of your mind controlling you and this will make all of the difference.

Let's take a brief look at those goals. Read over them and decide again if any changes need to be made. Make any changes and add any steps that you learned of. Now let's track your progress. Did you meet or exceed your expectations? If not then why not? If so then what lesson do you need to learn from it? Try to learn from the negative and the positive. If you did something that had a negative result, don't do that anymore. Also think about what you could do differently. If you did something that had a positive effect, think about how you can apply it to other things.

How did things go with your family and friends? Were you able to get some quality time in with anyone? If so, how did they respond to your progress? Do they think you are becoming someone else? While they may say it in a negative way, the truth is that you are becoming someone else. You are becoming a better you and that's always a great thing. Don't let the wind affect you now. Remember that you can love your family and friends, even if you don't buy into the negativity. Just be sure that you don't allow them to bring you down.

Lastly, how did you fare with helping others today? Were people receptive to your ideas? Did you plant any seeds? Did you feel like you were helping them or did you feel like you were pressuring them? This feeling is usually accurate so, if you felt like you were pressuring them, they may have felt the same way. Remember that people don't care how much you know until they know how much you care. Always make sure people know that you care before you say what you know. Keep that in mind as you end your day. How much better of a reaction would you get out of people if they knew you cared?

51

A STORY FROM MY OWN DAY
TWENTY-FIVE

D
ay twenty-five and I'm on the street early. I'm running and the pain has returned. I focus on the pain and it subsides enough that I barely even notice it. I have gotten pretty good at running with pain. So good that it affects my performance very little.

As I run, I let my mind wander to a friend of mine that recently passed away. He was a little younger than me and I knew him for most of my life. I wasn't able to attend his funeral, mostly because I didn't know it was taking place until afterward. I can only hope that everything was the way he would have wanted it to be and that he went out on his terms. Death usually makes me sad and this was no exception.

Death has a way of opening up our minds to things we would normally ignore or not think about. My thoughts turn to tomorrow morning. I fully expect to wake up and do my thing. Almost like I'm entitled to it or tomorrow is promised to me. The truth is, we have no idea when we will clock out. I have to wonder if my friend expected to wake up and do his thing. I decide to think hard about how I'm living and make changes that will leave everyone, including myself satisfied upon my death.

Enough about death, I turn my thoughts to living. I know that there are things that I want to do and things that I want to accomplish and I'm nowhere near ready to die, If I died tomorrow, I would leave a big mess for my family to clean up and that is not what anyone wants. I would also die with so much inside me and I owe it to myself and everyone else to get it out. It could be useless or it could be world changing but we will never know if I don't get it out before I die. I want to know that I gave this life everything I had. That I didn't let fear or the wind or anything else keep me from trying my best.

On day twenty-five, I learned that I have many more thirty-day challenges ahead of me and I'm happy for that.

52

DAY TWENTY-SIX

THE MORNING

On the morning of day twenty-six, I want to start out the same way we did yesterday. I want to establish a pattern that you can use after your challenge is completed. This pattern will change as time goes by, but it will help you keep the same feeling as you have right now. And that feeling that you have right now is a great one because you only have a short time left of your challenge. You also have momentum on your side and having a pattern will help keep it moving in your direction.

It's day twenty-six and you are even closer to completing your challenge. How does that make you feel? Do you feel like you thought you would feel? If not, it's ok. I'm not sure if you had clear expectations when you set out, but you do now. Try to set expectations for the end of this challenge. Also, I want to mention that your goals are important for many reasons. It's not just accomplishing the goals, its about who you become while you are trying to accomplish them. That's the real benefit. Setting and working towards goals will build you into something you never knew you could be.

Moving forward, let's take a few minutes and get ready to start your day. What attitude do you choose for the day? Make sure to set it now and decide that it will stay set. The wind is not allowed to affect your attitude, and neither is circumstance. Now decide to own the day and everything that comes your way. If it influences your day, you own it. If it has a negative effect, change it. If it has a positive effect, feed it. Now let's decide what to expect from our day today. Set your expectations at a level that will make you stretch but make sure it is achievable. Finally, relax. Feel that relaxed feeling for a moment and decide that you will feel this way every time you need or want to. Every time you feel like you are rushed, or your calmness is slipping away, remember to take a moment to relax and make a good decision.

I would like you to continue contacting friends and family today. Reconnect or visit with people you care about and share your recent journey. If they are interested, feel free to elaborate and tell them the details. Even the details that you aren't proud of. There is value in being a real person, even when it's not a shining moment and the value generally goes to the listener. Imagine if someone told you a real story about a relatable moment and they didn't spare the details, would you benefit from it?

And the last thing to do on day twenty-six, think success. You are what you think you are so why wouldn't you think about success. If you think that your world is going to fall apart, you will find a way to allow that to happen. If you think your world is about to explode with greatness, you will find a way to make that happen. Think success, not just for yourself but for others as well. When you see others, think that they are successful, even if you don't want to be where they are, they may be right where they are and therefor, they are successful.

The Afternoon

On the afternoon of day twenty-six, I want to start by asking you to take a moment and reflect on your challenge. Take a mental walk through the entire journey and see what sticks out. Are you happy with the journey so far? Do you wonder how you made it this far or are you confident that you could start over if you had to? The good thing is that there is no starting over. You have already learned many lessons and studied your own behavior so much that you now have an advantage over your cravings and urges. To say that you would be starting over wouldn't be accurate because you are so much farther ahead now that when you started.

Let's review your day again, how was your attitude throughout the day? How was your attitude at the end of the day? If it wasn't where you intended for it to be, why? Now let's move on to responsibility, Did you own the day? Were you able to own everything that affected you today? How did others react when they saw you take responsibility? Did they say that it wasn't anyone's fault? What about your expectations, were they accurate? Are they becoming more accurate as you keep trying? Remember that you will get better as you practice. Were you relaxed throughout your day or did you have to calm yourself? IF you had to calm yourself, what seemed worked the best?

Take a few minutes and re-read your goals, are they still accurate? If you need to make changes, now is a good time. What steps did you take today towards your goals? Were you able to accomplish what you expected? If not then what could you have done differently to meet your expectations? Remember that pursuing your goals will build you into a better you and that's a huge benefit all by itself.

Lastly, let's go over your family and friends activity from the morning. While you were connecting and catching up did you have any stray urges and cravings? How did it feel to connect with family and friends? Did anyone notice a change in you or did you play the part of the old you? If they did notice, did they consider it a positive change? If not, why? Is it just the wind doing its thing or did they not understand? This is about exposing yourself to the next wave of wind and cravings as well as learning to tell others about your progress. This not only helps you get better but may also help the person you are talking to. Remember to show that you care before you show what you know.

53

A STORY FROM MY OWN DAY
TWENTY-SIX

D ay twenty-six and I got a nice early start this morning. I have a little pain but it's barely even a discomfort at this point. It has been a rough week and even though I'm not a live for the weekend type of guy, I'm glad it's Friday. Weekends are more than just time off for me. I like to use the weekends to catch up and do the things that I wanted to accomplish during the week but couldn't. I am also looking forward to a little down time this weekend.

I'm running along and thinking about my next thirty-day challenge. I really want to do something that will make a difference. I've already decided what my next challenge will be but I also want to do one that will help others as well as myself. I'm not ready to nail down my second challenge but I have a few ideas in mind. I intend to do at least two consecutive challenges at once. I have a reminder on my calendar that alerts me daily, it says to do at least one thing that scares me. I have been seeing this reminder for so long that I hardly pay attention to it, but what if I actually did this for thirty days straight? What parts of myself would I change if I conquered my fear every day for thirty-days?

Another idea is to help someone in need for thirty days straight.

When I get focused in on my day, I tend to not see the suffering of people around me. Imagine the people I could help if I focused on that for thirty-days. Imagine how much better of a person I would become.

On day twenty-six, I decide to keep at least two challenges going all the time, or at least until I reach perfection. This may take a while!

54

DAY TWENTY-SEVEN

THE MORNING

H ere we are on the morning of day twenty-seven, with only three days left in your challenge. You may be both excited and a little worried about what happens next. The last few days, we have been a little repetitive because I want you to feel the similarity of the morning when this is over. You can always change this routine, but you will keep that same feeling for as long as you like. There are other variables involved but having a familiar feeling will help keep you on the right track. If you stopped smoking during this challenge, you don't want to start smoking again, ever but if you started running, you may want to switch from once per day to three times per week. Those are different examples that show how much different your path forward could possibly be.

Another thing to keep in mind about your challenge is the free time that you managed to carve out to do it. Not only did you find free time to complete your challenge, but you read this book, created an outline of your goals and read it daily. You also connected with family and friends, helped others find their way and performed many self-analyses along the way. Pretty impressive but what are you going to do with that free time now? We will work more on this over the next few days but for now, just keep it in mind.

Now let's get back to our familiar routine of creating our day. Put your attitude in the place you want it to be. Tell yourself that it will stay positive and won't be bothered by outside forces. Next, let's move on to owning the day. It's your day so decide now that everything that happens to you is owned by you. You own it so you can deal with it effectively. While you cant change everything that happens to you, you can own it and respond accordingly. Now set your expectations and try to be as accurate as possible. Remember to set the expectations of others, when the opportunities arise. Your goal is no surprises and no disappointment. And finally, remember to relax while you are going through your day. Relaxing will help you keep all of this together and help you meet your own expectations.

Let's read over those goals and decide what we want to accomplish today. What progress will you make towards your goals? Pick your steps and then stay with it. Don't let anything stop you from finishing what you choose. If you accomplish more than you expected, great but try not to miss your target. Somethings are beyond our control but make sure you give it everything you have. We never want to fall short on effort.

The Afternoon

Let's begin the afternoon by looking at your flame. How hot is it burning? Has it grown even more? Being determined is the gateway into success but mindset is key as well. We have been setting your attitude, owning the day, setting expectations and learning to relax in the mornings and now we will return to checking your flame in the afternoons. How did your flame react when you were staying positive and owning the day? When you were connecting with family and friends, did your flame grow even stronger? Maybe you hit a point where your flame flared up because you were setting an example for your family and friends. Setting an example is a win-win for you and the person observing the example. It makes both of you want to be a better person.

How was your attitude at the end of the day? Are you getting better at keeping a positive attitude? If so, what is strengthening your control? Is it practice or is there some specific reason that is helping?

Did you own the day and change the things that you can, or did you focus too much time on things that are out of your control? Where did you land on your expectations? Were they close? Are they becoming more accurate? How about relaxation, were you able to relax and make good decisions? And finally, did you act every time an opportunity was presented? I know we haven't been talking much about action for the last couple of days, but it is key to everything.

Now, let's cover those goals again. What progress did you make? Did you keep the expectations that you set for the day? Were you able to exceed your expectations or did you stop because you reached your quota? If you stopped because you reached your expectation, know that you should give it everything you have, even if you reach your quota, you should keep going. I know this sounds like a lot of effort and it is, but there will be days when you have less to give than the day before so if you are giving everything you have it will make up for those days. Keep pushing towards your goals, checking off those steps and making changes. Also, add any new goals as you go and prioritize them. Once you start achieving these goals and becoming the person you want to be, you will notice that your flame keeps growing. Remember to stop and enjoy the moment, every time you check off a step or goal. Progress towards your goals is a victory and you should celebrate these victories accordingly.

Let's talk briefly about the time management of your free time after this challenge, did you find a good way to spend that free time after this challenge? I won't try to influence what you do with your free time, but I will say that if you don't decide what to do with it, it will fade into daily activities and you will lose it. It will be soaked into social media, television and other low-level priorities, if you don't assign it to something. Moving forward, we will keep free time on our radar as we go through the day, this may help us capture it. I say again that there are many books and other sources to help you with time management.

55

A STORY FROM MY OWN DAY TWENTY-SEVEN

D ay twenty-seven was another early and painless run. As I am enjoying the early morning air and the feel of my feet hitting the pavement, I notice that I'm highly motivated and ready to destroy this run. I'm feeling great and I start to wonder if I can manifest days like this or if they just happen by chance or luck. I know the answer to this but maybe I don't yet know the formula for a great day. I believe luck is the stuff that unsuccessful people wait on. I mean, if great days are just lucky days then I may as well just sleep in until a great day comes along. That is meant to be a joke but many of us treat life that way. We wake up and decide that conditions aren't right for a great day, so we just allow the mediocre day to consume us. Instead of owning the day, we think or talk about what we wish we would have done. If I had only jumped out of bed and hit the street, I'd be feeling great right now. If it wasn't raining, I would go running. There are a million excuses we can make for ourselves, but the truth is we have to own the day. If we don't, the day will own us.

Great days may come to us by accident occasionally, but we also have the power to create them by having a plan and sticking to it. It's Saturday morning and I have already crossed off three things on my daily plan. Even though I started off sick and a little grouchy, It still feels great to get things done.

No one wants to feel like they didn't have what it takes, ever. Who wants to have to say that out loud? I didn't have what it takes, or I didn't own the day are terrible things to say. Who wants to say out loud that laziness got the best of me, so I didn't do what I wanted to? No one that I can think of would really want that but Many of us do it. My intention is to live fully every day. Take advantage of every day and make it great.

I turn my thoughts back to the importance of a plan. Imagine that it's a Saturday morning and you have many tasks that you want to accomplish today. Every time you get started on one, something happens to slow you down or stop you. After a few times, your mind is telling you to take a break and that no one should have to work in these conditions. If you are floating along, you may give in to this because it sounds like a good idea. If you have a plan for the day to refer to, you will crush this kind of thinking and keep going. It's the same for your life on a much larger scale.

On day twenty-seven, I asked myself if I want to spend my entire life being defeated by mediocrity and laziness or if I want to create each day and own it. I think you already know the decision I made.

56

DAY TWENTY-EIGHT

THE MORNING

Before we get started with our mindset on day twenty-eight, let's talk about the amount of time you think it will take you to finish your first three priority levels of your goals. How long do you expect it to take? Are your expectations realistic? Will you set deadlines or just work as hard as you can to finish them? I also won't try to tell you how to do this, but I will repeat Parkinson's law – "Work expands as to fill the time available for it's completion". This means that if you give yourself six months to complete your goals, it will take six months. If you give yourself a year, it will take a year. Some of us work better by not setting deadlines and just working hard. Again, I won't try to tell you how to tackle it, but I will ask you to never quit. Never give up, if your goals change and something doesn't fit anymore then change it and keep going.

Now let's move onto mindset, start again with your attitude. Decide to be positive and helpful. Don't let the events of the day or the wind choose for you. Next, decide to own the day and everything that happens to you. Decide to own what happens to others, even if you think it isn't yours. Moving on to your expectations, set your expectations where you want them to be and then strive to exceed them. There is an old saying that goes something like this "Most people don't aim too high and miss, they aim too low and hit". Keep this in mind when setting your expectations. Don't set them low because it's easy. Set them high enough so that you must strive to reach them. As promised, we will add free time to our daily routine. What are you going to do with it when this challenge is over? What are you doing with it now? How much free time do you currently have? You don't need to decide exactly what to do with it, but you should have it on your mind. Lastly, remember to relax, even when it seems impossible. Especially when it seems impossible, that's when it is most important to relax. When it seems impossible to relax, that's when poor decisions are made, relax and make the right decision.

Now let's read over those goals. Do you need to change anything? Do you need to add anything or any steps? If so, go ahead and do it now. Remember not to wait until you think you have them perfected, make changes and additions now. You can always change the changes but if you let them go by, you may lose them completely and there is no telling when you will get them back. After you have made your changes, decide what you will accomplish today. How much will you take on? Personally, I always bite off more than I can chew. That's how I keep myself striving and reaching.

I'd like you to revisit your challenge again today. Think back to the beginning and feel how hard it seemed. It seems much easier now but what changed? Did the thing get easier? Did your luck change? You already know the answer but I'm going to say it anyway, you changed. You have improved yourself, therefor, you will have more than you previously had. You have also mapped out your near future and developed the skills to continue mapping out your life forever.

Finally, as you start your day, think about your flame and what makes it flare up. What actions during the day make your fire burn hotter? When you find them, pay attention to them. Ask yourself what you like about them? What can you do to keep that fire burning? Feel around and determine if similar things also make your fire burn hotter. Remember that your determination is close to your passion so if something flares up your flame, you may be close to finding your passion. When you find your passion, your life will forever change.

Most people go their entire life and don't find their passion. Mostly because they never look for it. The wind blows them until they hit a spot where they can get a toehold, then they stay there forever. Never taking the chance of going against the wind or letting go of that toehold to reach for something better. Just living and dying in mediocrity. I find this to be very saddening and I hope you never do this.

The Afternoon

On the afternoon of day twenty-eight, let's begin with the same thing we started the morning off with. Your top three goals, did you decide how long it should take or did you decide to just go for it without a deadline? There is no wrong answer here, only a preference. Let's explore a little. If I told you that you had to dig a ditch that's one hundred feet long and three feet deep and three feet wide, how long would it take you? Do you have a pretty good idea, or would it be a wild guess? If you have no idea, I bet you could dig for an hour, do some calculating and then guess close but if I told you that you had to do it in three months, it may take you three months to do it. If you just started digging, it could take three days. On the other side of the coin, if I told you that you have three days to dig it and you had no idea, you may adapt and do it in the three days allowed. It's your choice how you want to look at it. Some people work better with a tight deadline and others just dive in and do it as fast as possible. You will know which method works best for you.

Now, let's recap your daily mindset. How was your attitude today? Are you getting better at keeping it where you want it? Keeping your attitude in the right place can be tough but it is well worth the time it takes to learn it. Being responsible is equally as important, did you own your day? Did you change the things that were in your control or did you focus on the things that you couldn't change? Did your day meet your expectations? Did you exceed your expectations, or did you stop at your quota? Were you able to relax and enjoy your day or were you tense and rigid all day? How about your free time, did you find time to think about it? Did you have any ideas about what to do with your free time after this challenge? Will you start another challenge?

Whatever you decide to do, in two days, you will need to start doing it, so be prepared.

How do you feel knowing that in two days, you will have completed your challenge? Are you tempted to finish poorly or are you driven to finish this strongly? Are you scanning over these last few days of text or are you being coachable? Are you looking forward to doing something different after this or will you miss this challenge? Again, ther are no wrong answers, just remember everything that you have overcome and keep learning and improving. It's that simple.

Now let's read over those goals and make any necessary changes. Add the things that you want and the steps that you will need to take. Look back over your day and determine if you put in enough effort or if you held back. If you held back, why? If you truly gave everything you have then take a moment to celebrate that. Giving your all is no easy task.

As we end the afternoon, look at your flame and see how it is reacting to the end of your challenge. Is it burning hotter than ever? If so, then why? If not, then Why not? I say again, pay attention to what lights your fire, it's more important than it seems.

57

A STORY FROM MY OWN DAY TWENTY-EIGHT

Again, on day twenty-eight, I'm running early and with no pain. My challenge isn't over but I can feel it creeping up on me. At this point, waking up and running is what I do and I can't imagine it any other way. The feeling of achievement and awareness before daylight is an amazing feeling and I've become accustomed to feeling it. I don't want to go back to the way it was before. Sleeping until the last minute and then sleep walking at work until nine am. I will leave that for others.

Since I'm close to the end of my challenge, I feel the urge to call it "good enough", to say that close enough is the same as finishing. Part of the reason I started this challenge was to become a better finisher and that's exactly what I will do. I will run this challenge like I just started on day one. My effort level will only increase as I near the end of this challenge. After it's over, Maybe I will even ramp it up for a few days to make a point to myself. Finishing will become a part of me from this point forward.

I have a lot going on in my life right now that requires much effort on my part. While it is becoming overwhelming. My effort will not fade. I will learn to deal with the things that are going on and continue to finish strongly. Momentum is on my side and my flame is burning hotter than ever. As I continue to run, I think about a quote by Og Mandino– "Failure will never overtake me if my determination to succeed is strong". I ask myself, am I strong and determined enough to get through everything that is going on and finish this challenge strong? The answer is a simple yes, said with absolutely no doubt or hesitation.

My current moment is not the moment of truth that will prove to me that I'm strong enough. This moment has me up and running at five am and loving it. This moment is great. The moment of truth is when my energy is low and my mind is trying to talk me into taking a break when I clearly don't deserve a break, and I still keep going. When I don't want to do something but I do it anyway, those are the moments that define me.

On day twenty-eight, I checked my determination. I learned that I have tons of determination when my energy is high but I need to keep learning to maintain my determination when my energy level is low.

58

DAY TWENTY-NINE

THE MORNING

Good morning on day twenty-nine of your challenge. Tomorrow is your last day, how amazing is that? One day left and you are off to your next adventure. As you prepare to enter that adventure, know that there is no set of rules to guide you. You will need to find your own way or follow someone else. It's ok to follow someone else, if that makes you happy but I doubt that it will. Creating your own path is a reward all by itself. I have walked my own path for years, so my memory of following is vague, but I doubt that I'd want to do it again. Following may seem easier but there is always that feeling of something missing. That unfulfilled feeling and sense of under achievement is enough to keep me away from the pack. You will decide if you will follow others of if you will create your own path and if you are happy, either way is fine.

As you prepare your mindset this morning, I want you to keep in mind that some experimentation in this area may be necessary. I want you to be familiar with the process that we have been practicing and be able to use it as a foundation, but I also want you to experiment as you go. Begin building this routine around you and don't ever be afraid to change it.

Now, let's get started. Get your attitude where you want it to be.

Decide how you will respond to the events of the day and how you will perceive everything. Next decide to own the day and all of the events, even if you can't change them. Remember to focus your efforts on the parts that you can change but own it all. You own it and you are responsible for it. Next, know what to expect and help others know what to expect. Set your expectation level and decide to exceed it. Remember to relax and handle every situation calmly. Next, think about your free time and try to come up with some ideas for it. And finally, make a promise to yourself that you will take advantage of all opportunities today by taking action.

Moving on to your goals, read over them. Make any changes or additions that you want. Next decide what progress you want to make today and ask yourself what could possibly stop you from achieving it? I hope your answer is that nothing will stop you. AS you go through your day of achieving your goals and succeeding, notice what makes things better and what makes them worse. Do more of the good things and less of the bad things and you will get better and better at achieving your goals. When you become great at achieving your goals, your determination will increase. Your flame will burn even hotter because you are completing your goals. Your goals are the path to your passion and if they aren't, they will become the path as you continue to develop them.

The Afternoon

On the afternoon of day twenty-nine, take a moment to feel great about making it this far. You are almost finished, and you should be feeling amazing. A little nervous about what to do next but still amazing. It's not quite time to congratulate yourself but the day is near. Take a few minutes and just feel it.

Now let's recap over your mindset for the day. Were you able to hold your attitude where you want it better than yesterday? Again, I don't want you to relive the past, but we can use it as a mile marker. When you look back to where you were yesterday, you may be able to see how far you have grown. Now look back at your level of responsibility, did you own the day? Were you focused on the things you could change or influence of did you complain about what should have happened and focus on the things out of your control? Remember you own all the parts of your day, so you get to choose what you focus on. At the end of the day, were your expectations met? Did you own those expectations as well? Did you work up to your expectations and stop or did you work until you had nothing left?

How did you fare on your goals today? Did you meet or exceed your expectations? Did you run into anything that you need to add to your list? Did you cross off any steps or goals that you may have accomplished? Do you still feel strongly about your goals or has anything changed? Do you feel like you are moving fast enough towards your goals or is something holding you back? What could you do to move faster? Are you talking to your mentors about your goals and progress? If not, it's a good time to start.

Let's move our attention to your flame of determination. How is it doing? Is it burning hotter than ever? Do you feel like you are determined enough to make it through your goals? When you think about your mindset, what does it do to your flame? Can you see the way to finding your passion yet? IF not, don't worry, it takes a while. I say again that some people never find theirs, mostly because they don't try. If you keep watching what makes you determined and working towards your goals, you will find your passion.

On day twenty-nine, I leave you with this thought. When you are dealing with issues that seem uncontrollable, Stop and remember how you defeated the cravings when they were still strong. This technique helps with almost anything. Stress, anger and frustration can all be dealt with in the same manner as you dealt with those cravings. Fins a place and close your eyes. Turn the background noise into something peaceful and think about the source. If you don't know the source, then search for it. When you find the source of the trouble, tear it apart. Completely dissect it. What makes it tick? What power does it have? Can it be controlled? Is it something I can change or is it something I need to learn to live with? Once you have it dissected, it loses its power and you can again gain control over your mind. Use this as often as you like, just remember not to rush through it. If you take your time and do it right, it works every time.

59

A STORY FROM MY OWN DAY
TWENTY-NINE

D ay twenty-nine and I'm on the street even earlier than usual. I am feeling a little pain, but the pain seems like an old friend that has come to visit rather than something awful. Mild to moderate pain seems to make the run a little more interesting at this point. Almost like a jalapeño pepper spices up dinner. I feel the end of my challenge creeping up and I want to be sure that I feel everything that I can possibly feel before it ends.

I think about how much different this is now than it was during the beginning of this challenge. Early in the challenge, my goal was to make the pain go away and, here, I am enjoying it. I have grown enough that the things that used to make me want to quit seem like a little spice to life. It's amazing how much we can change when we want to.

As I run, I turn my thoughts to the other activities that are going on in my life and I measure my growth in those areas as well. I find that I have grown but not as much in these areas as I have in the areas that this challenge have focused on. I find that there are two main reasons for this.

One I have put a lot of focus and effort into this challenge. I have measured and improved every step of the process in order to make this challenge a success. In other areas, I have used the adapt and overcome technique, which is effective, but it doesn't include focus, study and reflection needed to improve. In other words, I have spent more of my time on activities and less on myself, which is a poor and unsustainable method.

Secondly, I wanted this challenge to be a success. This challenge is something that I can out my whole heart into and that make a huge difference. In other words, I have passion for this challenge and when you have passion for something, it is in a class of its own.

On day twenty-nine, I imagined myself doing the things I have passion for and focusing on them intently. A great and somewhat intimidating picture began to form.

60

DAY THIRTY

THE MORNING

L et's begin the morning of day thirty by congratulating you for making it to the finish line. You have worked hard, overcame many obstacles and won battles to get here. I imagine your head is full of ideas and thoughts about what to do next. The good thing is that you can do the exact same thing tomorrow if you decide to do so. Another good thing about tomorrow, you can do anything you want. You can start a new challenge, double up on your goal efforts or develop a few positive habits. Anything you want, my recommendation is to find something positive and productive to fill the time you have been spending on your challenge.

Now, let's get your mind right. Choose your attitude before the day chooses it for you. Decide to be positive and not let anything change it. Remember that you will need to experiment with your mindset in order to make it your own. Next let's move on to responsibility. Decide to own the day and everything that comes with it. Now, lets set your expectation level and remember to set expectations for others as the opportunity arises. Think for a moment about your free time and what you will be able to use it on. Lastly, tell yourself to relax as you handle the day. Don't make knee jerk reactions, instead make smart relaxed decisions.

Now let's read over those goals and think about any changes that you want to make. Any goals or steps that you feel inclined to add, do it now. Next, decide how much you will accomplish today, and determine a plan to get it done. Think about how much you accomplished yesterday and what you could have done to accomplish more. How will you apply those thoughts to today's activities? I don't want you to live in the past, but it can be a good thing to glance back and search for lessons as you plan the day ahead.

The Afternoon

As we close out the day, I want you to focus again on what's next. What will you do with that free time that you recently acquired from the closing of your challenge? Will you fade back into your old routine? Will you spend your mornings gossiping and talking about what you could be doing? Will you spend it blowing wind at others that are trying hard to accomplish their goals or will you help them because you know how it feels to be in that position? It is important to fill the gap with something important. It's that simple. If you want to be wealthy, spend that time studying wealth. If you want to have even more time to spend, study time management. Spend your time wisely, it's more important than I know how to make it sound.

I ask you to recap over your attitude, responsibility, expectations, relaxation and free time as we always do. Take some time and think about whether you will do this daily after your challenge. What are the consequences if you don't and what are the benefits if you do? I will leave your mindset there on this final day. It will be up to you to follow up every afternoon and see how you did. If you write down a to-do list, read this book again or add a reminder to your calendar is up to you. Just remember to keep the momentum moving in the right direction and experiment often to see what works best for you.

Let's move on to your goals. How did you do today? Were you distracted with the end of your challenge? Were you able to defeat the distractions and accomplish what you wanted to? Did you work to your quota or did you give it everything you have? What will you do differently tomorrow? After all, tomorrow marks the start of a new you. A you that has been through so much and overcame obstacles that most people wouldn't dream of facing. A you that has built skills that will carry you into the future with purpose and confidence. You also have your roadmap laid out and the ability to change it as you need to.

As you follow your road map and work towards finding your passion, there will be failures that will test your commitment. These failures will be painful, but I want you to remember that failure is only a stepping stone. Failure is part of the process, but it isn't the end of the world. So, if you miss a goal or try and fall on your face, just dust yourself off and try again. If it feels like people are laughing at you, remember the wind and how it tries to blow out your flame. Protect your flame the same way you did before.

I will leave you with this final reminder. Never stop experimenting and changing. These methods that we have been doing are effective, but they may not be tailored exactly to you. You will find it helpful to mold the process around yourself. When the process is tailored to you, it will be easy but effective. When it is easy and effective, you will do it without spending energy, the process will flow naturally and effortlessly. Keep making smart changes and keep getting better and you will achieve your goals. When you achieve your goals, the wind will look at you in awe and believe you are cut from a different cloth than they are but you will know the sacrifice you made to get there.

61

A STORY FROM MY OWN DAY THIRTY

I t's day thirty, the final day of this challenge and I'm up and running early with no pain. It's a great feeling to be running on day thirty of this challenge because I'm about to finish something that is important to me. If I broke my leg right now, I would crawl around the track until my timer goes off. It sounds a little crazy but that's how much finishing this challenge means to me.

It's amazing how something as simple as running for thirty days straight can be so important to me. If I really think about it, this has little direct effect on my career or my personal life. None of my business family or my personal family care if I finish this challenge. If I had quit three days into it, they would have barely noticed, so why is it so important to me? The reason is simple, its because I want to. This directly affects me and everything about me. There is a saying that says "always work harder on yourself than you do anything else" and that's pretty much what I'm doing. Besides, if I were to quit this challenge, I would quit on pretty much anything.

Day thirty also brings a little sadness with it. This challenge has taught me many lessons and it has helped push me through many obstructions and personal laziness. I really don want to stop. I'm curious about how it will feel in the morning to wake up and not be committed to running. Will I go run anyway? Will I never run again after this? I'm pretty sure that I will be out here running again at five am or earlier.

On day thirty, I want to leave you with this – If you have been wanting to quit something or if you have been wanting to start a healthy habit, consider the thirty-day challenge. I know it seems too simple, but it has changed my life in so many ways. Changes way beyond getting up and running or even learning to finish. As I write this today, I am finishing another thirty-day challenge and two more will finish tomorrow. If you question my level of commitment, then I will also let you know that today is my wedding day. My wedding to the most beautiful woman in the world doesn't stop me from finishing my challenge so what will stop you?

On day thirty, I looked through a window into my future and there I was, a better version of myself and I was completing another thirty-day challenge.

Made in the USA
Coppell, TX
04 January 2025

43937557R00100